M000014922

TO
HELL
I RIDE

TO HELL I RIDE

WHEN A LIFE EXAMINED
BECAME WORTH LIVING

JASON CARTER

LIONCREST
PUBLISHING

TO HELL I RIDE

When a Life Examined Became Worth Living

ISBN   978-1-5445-2569-3 *Hardcover*

978-1-5445-2568-6 *Paperback*

978-1-5445-2567-9 *Ebook*

For you

The town of Telluride is named after *tellurium,*
a nonmetallic element found in gold. But historians claim
the town's name originated from callous heathens already
scarred by the frontier's sharp whip. These broken people
gathered to taunt fortune seekers headed to Telluride,
shouting "To-Hell-You-Ride!" because they knew
the mythical town's depraved and expanding underbelly
would devour their souls upon arrival,
just as it did theirs.

CONTENTS

1. HIT THE ROAD, QUACK 1

2. I SEE RED PEOPLE 19

3. A BEAUTIFUL SHAME 25

4. IN A GALAXY NOT FAR AWAY 33

5. HOOK, LINE, AND DRINKER 47

6. THE SON HARVEST 57

7. THE DEBASEMENT 65

8. CALIFORNIA'S COOLER 73

9. MIGHT AS WELL JUMP 83

10. HACK TO SCHOOL 103

11. WASHED OUT 111

12. SPRING LOADED 119

13. **YOUNG LIVES** *133*

14. **DETROIT SCHLOCK CITY** *143*

15. **A MIRE EDUCATION** *153*

16. **JIVEY LEAGUE MATERIAL** *163*

17. **THE SHAPES OF WRATH** *175*

18. **LOVE AT FIRST BLIGHT** *183*

19. **GUESS WHO'S NUMBING TO DINNER** *191*

20. **THE WEDDING INCEPTION** *201*

21. **START SPREADING THE BOOZE** *209*

22. **THE HOLLYWOOD SCUFFLE** *229*

23. **THE GOLDEN GRATE** *237*

24. **CAT AND SOUSE** *249*

25. **A SHIVER RUNS THROUGH IT** *261*

26. **DON'T DRY FOR ME, ARGENTINA** *269*

27. **CLASS ACT** *281*

28. **TURDS OF A FEATHER** *293*

29. **OUT OF FIN AIR** *301*

HIT THE ROAD, QUACK

"Do you think about killing yourself?" she asked.

Every time I cut carbs, I thought.

I credit my dad for conditioning me to slice intimate encounters in half by treating earnest questions as setups for distracting punch lines or gags, leveraging droll sarcasm, predictable quips, and the occasional spit take should my mouth be filled with wine.

But today, I bit my lip. Too bushed to stage my act. A rueful, long-running, one-person farce performed behind thick layers of self-deprecation, like a paint-caked wino working overtime in a circus dunk tank.

I cranked out raw material since learning to speak. Eager to test the latest in front of friends, strangers, and my unimpressed reflection in the bathroom mirror. But the woman questioning me now deserved better.

According to cocktail gossip, she graded out as the town's top psychiatrist. I estimated the bulk of her income came from my friends and acquaintances endorsing her. And since everyone in my circle carried on like merry crackpots, I expected little beyond my intake file getting rubber-stamped with whatever diagnosis represented her best guess.

Despite this, I elbowed my way into her oversold appointment book for an emergency session and handed her $350 for an hour of her time to uncover the reasons why mine ran out. I arrived at her office driving the straight-talk express. Because I couldn't live like this any longer.

So, I removed the shell protecting my afflicted sense of trust and coaxed this long-silent part of me to recap the curious details related to my morning jog.

Earlier, I pounded through a five-mile run. At the halfway point, I stopped. Not to catch my breath but to give suicide the considerable focus ending my life deserved.

On a familiar route, a pedestrian bridge draws over a busy highway. I rambled across this overpass countless times, always in the early dark of morning, on another fiendish hunt for a runner's buzz, driven mad to capture the immediate rush on the other side of the run's protective walls. And, in matters no less pressing, to sweat down the indicative red swells on my face expanding by the hour like super mutating tomatoes concocted in a lab.

But today, in the middle of the skyway, I slowed my grinder's pace down to a contemplative stroll, immersing myself in the eerie sights and sounds interrelated to observing perfect strangers getting on with their day. An infinite swarm of cars whizzing and zooming beneath my feet, disrupting the isolation I sought. A nomadic menagerie of glassy-eyed motorists, hollowed out by dread's sharp edges, all dashing like mad to a place or job they hated, to engage in demeaning activities with other folks also lacking the zeal required to slide out of bed unforced.

I came to a complete stop. My heart pounded against my ribs, beating faster than usual. I locked into the gradual slowing down of its tempo until the thump fell into a rhythm sounding measured and hypnotic. But far from calming. More evocative and lurid. Warlike and determined, audibly approaching like an unstoppable tank.

I visualized this killing machine rumbling toward my village, grinding up the road and flaming every creature and structure nearby into smoldering black soot. Each strike of my heart provoked thoughts related to cannon fire as the steady cadence and escalating volume of the discharges served to mock my inevitable doom. This, or a bummed-out boomer was burning down a joint in a car parked nearby, blaring "The Chain" by Fleetwood Mac.

A phantom boom left me deaf, standing in frozen silence, petrified. The air thickened, clotting into a murky syrup, now less breathable than bathwater. I gasped in all I could from the shock of wanting to fly off the bridge. A risky thing to lust for, primarily because my response to feverish itches, over time, evolved into an involuntary reflex I couldn't control—like a spasm, as impossible for me to stop as blinking, breathing, or extending my middle finger at whoever honked their horn.

I scanned the bridge for a suitable spot for a swan dive, but I called off the search. Too distracted by a sudden flash of brilliant colors streaking across the sky, like God himself opted to drybrush today's sunrise with atomic orange paint.

The abrupt urge to jump lost steam, deflating down to impotent shiftlessness, or what a groveling hack might describe as whole and earnest. Whatever I experienced transitioned me into a pacified state, comparable to being submerged in a volcanic ash mud bath at a spa east of San Luis Obispo.

Then a headlong burst yanked me out of the restorative slop like a pulled weed, chucking my body into an alternate existence. Now vibrant, brimming with conviction, and weightless, in full command of an inexplicably acquired set of superpowers, beckoning me to do the unimaginable. Move mountains. Fly around the sun. Or forgive Matt Damon and Ben Affleck for becoming overnight stars on the heels of a screenplay they contributed less writing to than the clerk at Kinko's who helped them print the first incomprehensible draft.

Before I doled out any miracles, I got shoved back into the sluggish reality of waking life. The place responsible for stripping me down into a vague shadow, now too detached to fear my upcoming flight. Finally, after three decades of unrelenting pursuit, the warmongers of my consciousness succeeded in corralling me, pinning me to the edge of my grim world's abyss. For once, I didn't bother with tap dancing.

Instead, I imagined the flight down. I visualized myself hovering, a brief pause before roundhouse-kicking Keanu Reeves's unresponsive face in *The Matrix* before accelerating downward like a shopping cart from Home Depot overstuffed with buckets of red paint.

I considered channeling the moxie circulating through a cliff diver's brass balls to execute a breathtaking twisting flip. What about mimicking something random and absurd? Like the robot. Or the first few choreographed movements of the Macarena. My parting gift to the listless commuters beneath me, somehow still hoisting themselves back on the hamster wheel for another go-around, desperate to find cause for cracking a smile, or, in the dreariest cases, to blink.

Would I die fast? Or worse, survive, hurling myself smack in the middle of another one of my life's cringe-worthy moments, which numbered in the billions? Only this time, I exceeded the embarrassment from the time I chatted up Jennifer Aniston at a bar in LA. I had her chuckling and blushing, right until I suggested we split and head to her place. "Um, yeah. No, thanks."

As a rule, Texas requires tobacco-chewing hicks driving massive, customized pickup trucks outfitted with grill guards weighing two tons and made of bone-crushing steel to exceed posted speed limits by twenty miles per hour.

It's a solid guess my last sight on earth would be an indestructible bumper welded to the front end of a broncobuster's hopped-up Dodge Ram. I pictured the childish truck bearing down on me like a screaming meteor before splattering my body into a cloud of red mist like a disfigured beet farmer's colostomy bag repurposed into a piñata.

The hayseed driving the truck might swerve, an upright citizen of God-fearing character, determined to miss what he mistook for a prized deer or a cold keg of Coors Light. As a result, his beloved truck would flip end over end at least ten times, causing one of those forty-car pileups I used to marvel at as a kid living in California watching *CHiPs* on TV after school. Not optimal.

But what if I somehow shirked death and survived? How would I handle losing the ability to walk, shower, or spoon-feed myself mashed bananas without the care provided by a maniac nurse found on the community corkboard at Whole Foods?

According to *60 Minutes*, nurses trolling for degrading caretaker jobs using pink flyers and thumbtacks do so because every hospital they worked for chased them off using pitchforks and torches. Now they're hell-bent on delivering a toxic dose of vigilante healthcare to a world plagued with rational assumptions regarding medical assistance. In terms of headspace, one mishandled bedpan is plenty to provoke the most unruffled self-advertised nurse into flavoring their sweetest patient's grilled cheese smoothie with strychnine before setting off on a nationwide killing spree.

Although once I calculated the physics of my situation (the height of the bridge, the speed of the traffic, and the extra twenty pounds of fat I packed on since Thanksgiving), the disagreeable care provided by an unhinged nurse crossed out as a nonissue since my immediate death added up to a mathematical certainty.

How would the news spread once I croaked? I didn't carry a license, only my phone, used for playing motivational songs to supercharge my toiling resolve. (Time to rethink my playlist?) So, let's assume the grisly aftermath correlated to a Siberian prison's mess hall after the inmates ran the chef through the meat grinder because he knocked over the week's only cauldron of borscht. How long until authorities identified me from the scattered bits and chunks of my flavorless corpse?

Of course, my family would flip out. I suspect a touch more than the day we found our pet goldfish, Floaty, on the kitchen floor below its bowl, locked in King Pigeon pose, stiffer than a lag bolt. But what dark, hellish road would my death send their lives racing down? Or, without me in the picture, would their lives improve? The way skin tends to mend after a boil gets lanced.

I fabricated a timeline metering my wife's grieving process. How long until she moved on and remarried? Five years? Ten months? Or would a lavish wedding reception designed around bottomless bottles of Veuve Clicquot and a surprise performance by Carly Simon singing, without a hint of irony, "You're so Vain" occur two hours after my wake?

Ugh. I couldn't stop myself from considering the eager little bore taking my side of the bed. No doubt this poacher is a gentleman—a devout, churchgoing man. He gets community kudos for being a salt-of-the-earth type with a good heart. His biggest sin involved pencil-whipping a scorecard the only time he played Pebble Beach. The cooked-up score of eighty-nine hangs on his office wall, like a pesky albatross, examining his character from a coastal-chic frame created with driftwood sourced from the beach below the course. In quiet moments, he allows himself to relive the round, running through the contracted numbers scrawled across the mucky scorecard, his cheeks burning red-hot with liar's shame. But this is a good thing, proof he's not a homicidal sociopath, just a hack troubled by the steadfast integrity of simple math.

In a lucky twist, he's also a widower. His wife died two years ago from either the most aggressive case of pancreatic cancer on record or sheer boredom. So, he's left to offering his able best to the essential duties of raising two kids without a loving partner. The son is an uptight high school jock gripped by the political spectrum's far-right side. The other child, his daughter, is a bookish sophomore at Brown. She dabbles in designer drugs and gender neutrality and subscribes to *The Nation,* making her the only person in my wife's new family worth chatting up at a cocktail party or on a plane. Well, if I lived, of course.

A few years back, he sold his uncomplicated small business for a fortune. The company sold fracking sand around the Texas panhandle for $10,000 a load. Now the lonesome twit needs a beautiful partner to travel the world flying private while burning through his hoard of cash, which only grows, like an aggressive fungus with no cure.

For my wife's sake, I hope he's a decent chap and more dependable than a Kohler toilet's sweet flush. But he can't be a rugged dreamboat, like an early '90s Kevin Costner, a man accustomed to turning heads in every room entered. I'm fine if he's an everyday Joe squared up with the IRS and owns a second home in the mountains or on the coast. In a perfect world, his biggest problem dwells in the thirty pounds of fat he packed on grief-bingeing Ding Dongs by the carton after his wife went tits up.

As a point of personal vanity, he must be bald or balding, and seeing his hair clog the shower drain every morning makes him cry like a baby touching a red-hot stove.

But here's the deal. The man replacing me wouldn't matter. He could be a Doak, an Alan, or a swinging hairy slimeball named Barry. Because Meryl Streep pings Steven Seagal for acting tips before my wife loves this clown as much as me. Well, like, before our second year of marriage, at least.

Oh, hell. What about my beautiful kids? How would they handle him? I hated hoping they'd mock him, snicker behind his back, and keep a running gag going around misplacing his wallet and car keys. At least in the beginning, before warming up to his straitlaced, no-nonsense charms in due time, which they would.

If I exhibited a living purpose, it materialized in being a love-struck father absorbed in raising kids to be loving, wise, and mature, well beyond their years. As a result, they trust life's wonky process and understand that every event—including disagreeable ones like striking out, losing a pet, or hearing your old man did a belly flop off a bridge into oncoming traffic—is a distinct gift from the cosmos, wrapped in existential meaning.

I taught them, no matter what, life's flow reveals hidden pathways to the predestined places where a cheering universe awaits their arrival. A sharp pang reminds me I failed to explain that if they found themselves loitering on freeway overpasses plagued with compulsive yearnings to fly, to go ahead and scoot on across to the other side.

At some point, I bought a life insurance policy, but not enough. At best, the payout covered two years, including a rushed remodel of the master suite, a Range Rover, and the healing thrills of a Disney cruise. But I suspect the policy's payout didn't honor backflips off bridges onto highways.

What about all the bills? I handled those online, never thinking to share my clunky process or birdbrain passwords, which I scribbled on five-by-seven-inch cards duct-taped to the inside of a three-ring checkbook. Resulting in a jumble of unsystematic numbers (favorite running backs) and meaningless words (dubious nicknames like Hoover, JJ Manners, and, er, Cocktail) scratched down at different times, using various pens, which gave the puzzling data points no evident connection whatsoever. Only gibberish. The outpourings of a demonic child, all tossed when my desk got cleared out because the handlers thought my batty ledger was Damien Thorn's Christmas wish list.

Without Robert Langdon from *The Da Vinci Code* snooping through my life's sordid history for clues to crack the idiot's riddle, my family would lose electricity and water, and soon start receiving matter-of-fact letters delivered in unsettling pink envelopes from the bank about our mortgage and overdrawn accounts. Can embarrassed ghosts send sorry notes?

I imagined the indifferent scene at my funeral. Over a hundred people? Some disappointing no-shows. An old friend traveling on business or suffering through his noodle-legged kid's soccer tournament in Overland Park, Kansas. And a professor who had misread me, incorrectly labeling me with promise.

Instead, a boneheaded executive from work turns up after picking the short straw during a leadership meeting. Here to show a company face, calling attention to the amount of grief felt by my colleagues, who collectively elected to hang back at the office for unsupervised Instagram scrolling and breakroom grab-ass.

Damn. I should've penned a poignant note to my wife and kids, or produced a confessional video, like Michael Keaton shot in his critically panned flop *Life*. Even if I lost all sense of artistic dignity (or otherwise) and recorded a cornball opus, the final cut, I imagine, would've elevated *Life* above *Citizen Kane* on every film critic's list.

I cringed, imagining the laughable video shot on the cheap, like a snuff film, with me blabbing into the screen, spewing out frantic tidbits of clichéd wisdom I picked up along my life's cluttered path with a trash spike.

Be cool to waiters. Never talk during movies. Um, don't jog over skyways if your insides are rotted pitch-black with depression.

A middle-of-the-road minister who I scattered from in public like he was a religious terrorist strapped to a bomb suit would read the benediction, dropping in biblical quotes less relatable to my life's story than if Rudyard Kipling's poem "If—" were read aloud at a boll weevil's retirement party.

I'm sure he would turn in a workmanlike performance, reading the same "better place" script he wrote for a funeral the week before (a novice, middle-aged biker flattened by a school bus).

Who would get scapegoated with the unsettling task of speaking on my behalf? Hopefully, my father-in-law, a man I love and admire maybe more than my own. He's a worldly and affable man of the people, regionally famous, and his ability to connect with a crowd strips Oprah Winfrey's interpersonal chops down to Joaquin Phoenix's portrayal of the Joker.

Also, I trust in his exceptional talent to pivot the frosty attention away from my gruesome suicide (closed casket) by serving up an amusing anecdote about the time he played polo with a third cousin of a Saudi prince. An amusing recap sure to warm up the room's chilly mood.

Next, with the lights dimmed, a dismal photo montage would start projecting onto a makeshift screen, showcasing a mishmash of stock pictures taken during my ordinary life. Look, I'm standing on the pitcher's mound in Little League. I'm holding a tuna caught at sea! Followed by an embarrassing sequence of boilerplate bro poses: tipsy with friends in high school, drunk with fraternity brothers in college, bombed with roommates after college.

Then, thankfully, a series of images charged with meaning. My wedding (four hundred guests!), the day I married my dream girl. Sure, the dubious double-breasted tuxedo came from a rental shop, but the smile on my face amounted to the most genuine one I ever wore, and I owned this smile, mine, to wear forever, seemingly.

To the relief of those in attendance, the languid pace of inter-linked images speeds up, showing me in three different hospital delivery rooms holding each of my newborn kids. The wondrous exhilaration on my face shows, but the pictures are a billion miles from capturing a microscopic particle of the real, transcendental bliss incinerating my insides like a nuclear blast during these magical moments.

Oh, the picture of me after acing hole number one at the Country Club. I'm standing on the green, holding the flag like a moron leading the world's worst parade. An incredulous smile cuts across my face, as if I passed an exam I didn't study for. The rest of the slideshow maintains its predictable, uninspired theme. A few throwaway snapshots of me doing something "interesting" or "adventurous." Behold! I'm leaning against a hot dog cart, braving the "gritty" streets of New York. Now I'm skiing down a mountain sheeted with more mud than spring snow.

Since I lived in South Texas, whoever cobbled the "tribute" together made extra sure to include a befitting portrait of me squatting next to a dead deer. A real sweetheart of a Kodak moment. My hands and clothes are stained with blood, and the pained expression on my face denotes the frenzied guilt of a reluctant serial killer, yet here I am, holding up this magnificent creature's decomposing head like a winning keno card.

What song would prop up this flimsy clip show? My first choice would be Warren Zevon's "Poor Poor Pitiful Me." This tune communicates an ideal blend of punchy irony matched with a subtle and sardonic style, all held together by a catchy chorus people might jump up and sing along with. Next in line, my other favorite troubadour, Tupac Amaru Shakur. How about a little "Heavy in the Game"? For this starchy crowd? A stretch.

Besides, if I attended the funeral of a forty-four-year-old white guy who did a belly flop onto a freeway and "Heavy in the Game" backed his milquetoast montage, the intensity of my laugh would make Max Cady from *Cape Fear* so uncomfortable he might jump up and run, screaming toward the exit.

If I got to play DJ, how could I not pick "Learning to Fly" by Tom Petty? A song ripe with the flimsy sort of metaphysical irony shaping my malignant worldview. The breached musical delivery of my last stillborn joke. No surprise. Anytime I expected a knowing wink or cognitive appraisal for my abstract comedic shenanigans, people responded with blank stares, troubled silence, or asking a party's host for a different seat at the dinner table.

Provided the song "Desperado" by the Eagles played no part in my funeral, my wobbling legacy lugged a puncher's chance of not becoming a total joke, cosmic or otherwise.

Back on the skyway, as the cars and massive pickups raced below me to nowhere, I found my breath and started to jog, leaving the trash heap of irrational thoughts of suicide behind me. Again.

Back in the therapist's office, I looked at her and said, "So, yeah. I think about it. Suicide. But not for real, more like seeing a mirage," I said.

The esteemed psychiatrist, my own Dr. Lowenstein, stayed silent, scribbling notes in her journal—and took her sweet-ass time doing so. Long enough, I suspected, to jot down the myriad of red flags observed and underline, three bold times, a reminder to call—the second I walk out the door—a white van equipped with a cage and driven by stout men. Either this or her list of things to do before visiting her deadbeat son in Portland needed tweaking. Whatever the case, when she finished writing, she put the pen down and closed the journal.

She worked herself through a deep and measured breath, then raised her eyes, striking mine with piercing, unflinching focus. They shimmered with curiosity, not sweet and childlike, but authoritative, more agitated than bemused. It's like she stumbled across a glitch in nature's matrix, now forced to scrutinize me, the way an owl perched on a barn's rooftop would, deliberating the reasons why a common pig attired in a tuxedo stood in the slop, plucking his way through Niccolò Paganini's "24 Caprices" on a Stradivarius violin.

At last, she blinked. "Well, Jason, you can't drink anymore."

Three days later, I loaded up my Suburban for a family road trip to Colorado. In regular times, heading to the mountains with my family filled me with immense joy. But in the days leading up to departure, I kept hearing her words in my head. Incredulous, I listened with the focused intent of a shifty lawyer pursuing bogus loopholes. If I determined a trace of doubt in her voice, I could spin her speculative assessment into a plausible enough reason for the judge to toss my guilty verdict in the courthouse trash.

Well, Jason, you can't drink anymore.

Conversely, in truth, the confident mobilization of these directive words triggered an unexpected tingle of joyful preservation, kindred to a wilting castaway's rosy reaction upon recognizing the sound of a rescue boat's blowing horn. *I'm saved, Princess Coconut! I mean, uh, we're saved!*

Still, overall, I clung to shadowy reasons to keep myself offended and furious. Who did she think she was, a brilliant psychiatrist dedicated to saving people's lives? The nerve!

As things stood, it didn't matter if I felt giddier than a rave kid licking a ketamine lollipop, or more bent than a screenwriter draped in a green Starbucks apron. Because in the end, her disagreeable words coerced me into mulling through my pseudo-tragic history and addressing the distressing questions about my immediate future.

Why did I drink the way I did? Could I ever stop? And what if the skyway I ran over on most mornings lacked the safety wrapping of an impenetrable chain-link fence?

At five in the morning, with the Suburban packed, I poured a jumbo coffee for the road. The drive from my house to Telluride's city limits takes seventeen hours. Thinking of the long haul ahead made me groggy, suddenly vulnerable, and hypercognizant of my breached perspective.

I sat brooding in the driver's chair, feeling condemned, as if I had just gotten sworn in by a hanging judge in advance of getting cross-examined by a bloodless, Ivy League–educated cyborg—a theatrical drubbing I expected to last the duration of the trip.

I cranked up the Suburban and pulled out of the carport and onto the street. While I adjusted the rearview mirror, I caught a glimpse of my precious kids in the back. Each one wrapped in a blanket, sleeping like chipper cubs in a cozy and well-protected cave.

I caught the reflection of my own face, which appeared waxlike and smudgy. Pale skin, dull and lifeless eyes. The empty likeness of a face more suitable if it were attached to a man rotting in a casket, not behind the wheel of a two-thousand-pound truck loaded with loved ones about to haul off on an extended, multistate drive.

I took a deep breath and marked the time—5:03 a.m.—then shifted down into drive and pressed on the gas, now trekking to Telluride and, also, a side trip of my own, deciding earlier to split off and take the less-traveled route down memory lane. A meandering and gnarly detour I feared taking for the same reason I never enlisted in the Marines, bought a talking parrot, or stayed at a Sandals Jamaican Resort—to avoid, at all costs, the things God designed to snap a man's will to live in half like a toothpick.

But a telling surge of daring chills clarified the murky purpose behind my compulsive voyage. Settled and more desensitized than trusting, the wheels of retrospection started rolling, taking me to the first of many flashbacks on this drive straight to hell.

I SEE RED
PEOPLE

At the absorbent age of six, my mom told me a story about my dad and his fraternity brothers. Unfortunately, if her objective centered around scaring me straight, her colorful narrative fell short, missing the mark by a distance measured in parsecs.

That's because hearing the tale led me to believe my dad came to earth from another planet, kept a red cape hanging in his closet, and could leap over tall buildings in a single bound.

In 1968, my mom and dad, wide-eyed newlyweds, found a shoebox-sized apartment in Lincoln, Nebraska, to call their first home. For context, any living creature in Nebraska, human or otherwise, elevates Cornhusker football above all else: rain, a prime steak, and the folksy comedic leanings of Johnny Carson.

Sure, people living in Texas and Alabama boast their devotion to football borders on religion. Well, in Nebraska, courts use the football season's preview book to swear in witnesses before testifying during a trial.

Every home game sells out and has since the Cuban Missile Crisis, which, coincidently, took place during football season. So nobody in Nebraska ever heard about Castro's nuclear game of cat and mouse.

But in a state where everyone's grandma knows more about the team's third-string quarterback than the shiny-chested hunk bonking every character living inside their favorite soap, my dad's obsession with Big Red football stood out.

My mom's feel-good story took place in the fall after graduation, on game day. With the team playing the Buffaloes in Boulder, my parents made plans with two couples to host brunch and listen to the game on the radio. But as the sun started rising, a wild mob of my dad's fraternity brothers rammed a full keg through their front door.

Right away, they started mixing tomato juice and beer into glass mugs, screaming, "Go, Big Red! Go, Big Red!" Before my mom could run them off with a steak knife, my dad assumed the pole position and was already guzzling down every sudsy, glorious drop of red-colored beer from his own oversized mug.

As a six-year-old boy, I listened in wonder, hanging on every word, projecting vivid images of my dad building momentum toward ramming speed, which made me blush with runaway pride. My dad. The alpha. Knighted as the pack's undisputed leader. An ultimate man's man inspiring his brothers, not with fleeting words but through the irresistible powers of physical demonstration.

I imagined the elusive positivity embedded deep inside his intricate personality unlocked and radiating, pulling anyone around him in like a tractor beam, imposing his will, commanding them to slam down a thousand beers dyed red before kickoff and bask in the glory of their blessed lives. Just once more. Before life forced them to break rank and scamper off to law school, slide a bank-breaking rock up their sweetheart's plump ring finger, or get dumped into dense jungles on the other side of the earth, left to fight armed strangers with guns, grenades, and their shaking hands.

When the game started, emotions ran wild. The boys roared at explosive plays and cursed blue streaks at bobbled snaps and yellow flags. Fists pounded tables, feet kicked over mugs full of red beer, and knowing my dad, if the other team scored or moved the chains on third and short, his eyes rolled back, and he howled like a steer getting his skull popped open with a captive bolt pistol.

By the end of the first quarter, my mom stormed out, hoping to find a mortal and functioning group of humans watching the game in an environment less like a prison rec room after the inmates slaughtered the guards.

Later, hours after the game ended, she returned to the apartment. From outside the door, to her surprise and relief, she didn't detect a peep. Total silence. But when she opened the door, she screamed, reacting like a weekend camper finding Bigfoot taking a dump in her tent.

The floated keg stood upside down in a trash can. And ten thousand crushed cans of Pabst Blue Ribbon covered the floor as if a delivery truck had fallen through their roof. Only a few men remained, but the few and the proud who did looked dead, sprawled out across the floor or slumped over furniture, twisted up in grotesque positions as if they'd been deboned. Each stained bloodred and soaking wet from head to toe, making my mom think Charles Manson and his flower-power pals dropped by to cheer on the team before things got weird.

But within this hellscape, she sensed the odd presence of hope, signaled by a familiar scent drifting above the lingering game-day stench. This curious aroma carried notes related to virtue, both clean and sturdy. Suggestive of unsoiled winter snow or a kitchen sink bubbling over with soapy froth. Indeed, this fragrance matched the aromatic profile of fresh starts and ruddy new beginnings.

In many cases, a single whiff ferried the influence to calm frazzled nerves and restore faiths shattered by circumstance, like when a barn burns to the ground, or an F4 tornado grinds up a record-setting crop the night before harvest.

The pungent bouquet epitomized the unwavering attributes hardwired through the people of the heartland, reminding them that in tough times, they shouldered enough gumption to keep moving forward with one eye glued to the eastern horizon to witness the sunrise, once again, rising out from the earth's cruel dust.

Finally, the mysterious origins of the beautiful stink struck her, like a romanticized thrust ramming through a barricade obstructing recognition. And she smiled, relieved, opening herself to the neural strokes of fresh paint.

Brimming with hope, she sashayed into the kitchen to see all the miracles performed by the ceremonial unleashing of flat-coated latex paint. Again, she screamed, only this time for real.

Indeed, an open pail of fresh paint sat on the floor, but a football -ogling beast had kicked the bucket over, puncturing the sides with deep dents, indicating the can withstood multiple blows administered with unnecessary additional force. More alarming, the paint pooling on the floor and dripping down the wall was the color of warm blood, as if my dad and his buddies reshot the shower scene from *Psycho*.

Decades later, like everyone else, I soaked up the flood of gory images captured at OJ Simpson's Brentwood estate splashing over the front page of every paper on earth. I wondered if seeing the bloody walkway leading up to the Juice's front door made my mom misty with nostalgia, bringing her back to their modest newlywed kitchen. I'm thinking a hard no.

So, what happened? Well, before they passed out, my dad and his fraternity brothers honored the team's win by painting their white refrigerator (a wedding gift) Cornhusker red, using dishrags and a basting brush. Taking my own liberties to picture my mom's reaction, it's a shame my dad and his pickled brethren didn't have a buddy waiting in the driveway behind the wheel of a white Ford Bronco, coked to his eyeballs and ready to outrun a thousand cops (and my livid mom) on their merry way to Mexico.

At the time I processed this story, I loved the movie *Star Wars* more than anything on earth. I also came across a movie called *Animal House* on this new thing called cable. And the combination of my dad's story and the moment Eric Stratton bounced a Wilson golf ball off Neidermeyer's head detonated an intoxicating dream bomb inside my undeveloped brain.

This surprise attack blew *Star Wars* to the back of my mind. Allowing for the emergence of a new path leading me to the promised land. A mythical place where grown men drank beer for breakfast, college football outflanked religion, and white refrigerators got sacrificed in thy team's honor.

I couldn't wait.

A BEAUTIFUL
SHAME

I came out of the womb possessing a live right arm, and every coach I played for after T-ball plunked me on the pitcher's mound. In Little League, at the ripe age of nine, I got bumped up to play with eleven- and twelve-year-old boys.

This plump of red dirt became my front-row seat in life's cathedral. For the most part, my family sidestepped church, relegating the pitcher's mound to the only place I dared pondering the long-shot possibility that God existed and might even be watching my back.

When I addressed the mound before a game, I compressed the ball in my throwing hand and spun it like a snow globe, envisioning the barrage of sharp sounds popping off stretched cowhide striking the catcher's glove like a bullwhip. In these moments, I caught the quickest glimpse of my purest self in an elusive mirage before it vanished, as always, with the same sudden and earthy permanence of a falling star plummeting behind a glacier.

As my arm heated up, the pops off the glove escalated in amplification and cadence, creating an auditory equivalent of Rocky Balboa punching a slab of beef hanging from a hook as the movie's theme song echoed between my ears.

And speaking of echoes, some of my dad's quirks started ringing in my skull like bell-tower clangs. For example, he mumbled to himself, shirked affection, and with increasing frequency, drank more beer in a single afternoon than the Pittsburgh Steelers polished off after winning the Super Bowl.

But the man loved playing catch. We tossed the ball back and forth most nights when he got home from work, which taught me to throw strikes blindfolded.

To me, when we played catch, I chose to think my dad acknowledged something distinctive enough in me worth fostering. This intermittent belief muted out the regular thunderclaps heralding his advancing peculiarities as a father. At least during the hazy, soft-focused minutes while playing catch.

Each day after school, I waited for him to pull up from work. Stooped in the yard or perched inside by the window holding a ball and two gloves. When his car swerved in, I hopped up like a dog anxious for a walk. Once my arm got loose, he crouched down like a catcher, and I progressed through a full windup (mirroring Nolan Ryan, who played for my nearby Angels) before rifling the ball with a hiss, making a quick trip to the back of his glove, which never had reason to reach outside the tight boundaries marking the strike zone.

When he worked late or zoned out during college football, I threw a tennis ball against the garage, using the metal lift handle to establish a microscopic strike zone. I never paused to consider my family inside, forced to endure hours of the deafening racket generated from the ball crashing into the garage's paper-thin surface. I only pictured my dad sitting inside, grinning like a child at a magic show, cheering each boom of the ball like a gullible twit. *Again. Again. Do it again!*

More believable is how every fiftieth thwack reminded my dad to check the fridge and assess if enough beer remained to pull him through another agonizing afternoon in suburbia, trapped in hell.

Looking back, I hate speculating pitching against the garage turbocharged his early-stage problems with booze. That would imply I lured him to the edge of reason before donkey-kicking him down the slippery path leading to full-blown alcoholism.

I remember reading the popular books written by Judy Blume in the late '70s. She reported on the lush intellectual landscapes developing inside the minds of young girls. But if she penned a simpler story, say, about a boy, an overthinker keen to spin his father's unfeeling, slushy transgressions into proof points indicative of a paternal love, a fitting title might be *Are You There, Dad? It's Me, Target.* But what do stupid kids know?

A giant beast played on the first-place team in our league. We called him Big Donny. As a twelve-year-old boy, he possessed the build of a full-grown ape, and he led the state in baseball's most definitive statistical categories, including home runs, batting percentage, and biological reasons to wear an adult-sized jockstrap.

When everyday kids from earth hit an incoming pitch, the ball bounced off the bat with the spring-load of a soiled dishrag and bored through the air like a leaky water balloon launched from a wrist-rocket salvaged from a toy store's trash. But when Big Donny made contact, the ball shot off the bat like a shoulder-fired missile aimed at an overhead airliner cruising at thirty thousand feet.

The last time we played Donny's team, they smacked us around the field as if we ran off with their orange slices and Gatorade. And Big Donny launched two moonshots, last seen streaking over Tijuana.

The next time we faced them, the coach penciled me down to pitch. My teammates, plus the parents from both teams, made sure to communicate how humiliating this outing would go.

Before trotting out to the mound, the coach pulled me aside, advising me to throw everything outside or in the dirt when Donny stood over the plate. This way, he figured, Donny couldn't blast a line drive through the wiring connecting me to a sustainable human existence.

When Donny came to the plate, the crowd in the bleachers leaned in like bug-eyed tourists bunched around the lion's cage at feeding time. My catcher held his glove below his knees and far enough outside to scratch the next batter's balls. He punctuated his heedful message by jabbing at the dirt as if a buried bomb ticked underneath the left side of the batter's box.

I had no intentions of bailing out. Not a chance in hell. Besides, other than the blurry outline of Donny's hulking body hogging the plate, from the mound, all I saw in crystalized Technicolor was the metal handle from my garage jutting out of my hysterical catcher's chest.

I found rare comfort in the absolute clarity of things, as defined by the indisputable outcomes determined by the dogged rigors of science: the earth is round, water freezes at thirty-two degrees, and I could peg the metal handle screwed through my garage from forty-six feet on my knees with both eyes closed.

I waved off my catcher flapping both arms in the direction of the ground. *No thanks, pal.* I had little interest in braiding Donny's back hair. I showed up to play some damn ball.

I caught Donny looking with my first pitch. A whistling heater with less bend than a steel pipe. And why wouldn't he be looking? He deemed the likelihood of receiving a hittable pitch from the nine-year-old upstart—let alone one piercing through the meaty guts of the strike zone like a sniper's bullet—as the same as getting offered the role of Tinkerbell in his school's production of *Peter Pan*. Strike one.

He stepped back. Surprised and bemused, reacting the same way a lion at the zoo might if the antelope carcass rotting in his cage hopped to its feet and started break dancing. He offered me a sporting grin, which failed to mask his rage boiling underneath the macho hairs sprouting out from every visible space on his arms and face. I suspected he thought facing me would be less taxing than playing pepper with his sister using a volleyball and a boat oar. I disagreed, striking him out twice.

On his final at-bat, he came to the plate steaming more than a Chrysler Cordoba overheating on the way to Palm Springs, swinging for next week. But he popped up an off-speed pitch, a slow floater, too limp to push through the shallow part of right field. And the ball fell into the fielder's glove like a rolled-up pair of cotton socks fresh from the dryer. Game over. We won.

The game's scorecard accounted for the only pitch thrown outside the strike zone. A beanball I fired at Donny's ear to brush him back off the plate.

Donny's dad coached his team and held the title awarded to the meanest prick in the league. An unapologetic military type boiling under a wiry crew cut, gifted at treating kids (and their parents) like day-one grunts starting boot camp. If a baby-faced kid bobbled a routine grounder or struck out looking, his head exploded like the television anchor reading the news in *Scanners*.

After the game, he charged toward me at a brisk, robotic clip. My mouth dried up with panic. And before I could scatter, he got in my face, extended his hand, and smiled. "Great game, kid.

You're a real bulldog," he said.

His favorable words of validation exceeded any compliment I ever received from a grown man. Or anyone, really.

I swelled up with a startling degree of emotion and pride, coming close to tears. "Thank you, coach," I said.

"Doesn't mean we won't whip your ass in the playoffs." He chuckled and moved on, leaving me speechless with self-belief.

Of course, at the time, I didn't recognize what any dime-store psychologist would've spotted through heavy fog from a mile away. The atypical magnitude of my reaction is best described in the groundbreaking article "Kill Them All," written by Carl Jung.

In it, he proposed disconcerting behavior in undistinguished children resulted from the conspicuous lack of paternal validation, verbal or otherwise. Furthermore, the trailblazing healer argued these dicey youngsters represented modern society's worst nightmare—one thousand times more threatening to humanity than the Spanish flu, socialism, and moving pictures combined. And unless the world united to find, trap, and exterminate every child weighed down with emotional baggage, citizens inhabiting earth would vanish in a murderous apocalyptic hellfire beset in juvenile angst.

But, oblivious to his revolutionary findings, I stumbled around after the game in a happy trance, too delirious to decode the air-raid horn's screams, alerting me, and people like me, to dive for cover because enemy bombers were in flight and approaching fast.

IN A GALAXY
NOT FAR AWAY

I n 1978, Jimmy Carter lived in the White House, *Grease* ruled the box office, and I reigned as the king of second grade at Valencia Elementary in Laguna Hills, California.

Two years earlier, my family moved there by way of Nebraska. No offense to Nebraska, home of the good life, but to a kid my age (and twenty million other people), California represented the coolest place to be on earth. Anywhere else reminded me of a pediatrician's waiting room or the bedding department at Sears.

One summer, we traveled back to Nebraska, and I fell sick into a series of severe allergy attacks. My eyes watered, burned, and itched. Sneezing hurt, making me think fleshy chunks of lung tissue gusted out with the seedy germs blasting from my mouth each time my body contracted after a snotty expulsion.

Since I checked out as a healthy kid, these lethal maladies puzzled me, and no amount of medicine made a bit of difference. To which my dad, with the passive assurance of a small-town physician, said, "We need to rush you back to the smoggy Southern California air."

I smirked with pride. For once, the reassuring hands associated with being rooted in the earth's soil gave me a squeeze. Born by lucky chance at Camp Pendleton, but never being told what counted as home, I identified as a California kid now, carved in stone, right down to my body's physical rejection of oxygen floating around in the other forty-nine states. And I needed to race back to my birthplace before this clean, country bumpkin air caused my organs to explode.

I loved my school and made tons of friends. I captained the organized teams I played on outside of school and always got picked first when makeshift teams forged together on playgrounds. The girls liked me too. Including the older ones in the fourth grade. I figured this out when I kept getting gushy notes passed to me saying as much. But most gratifying of all, I found my first, one-and-only best friend, a kid named Doug.

I can't classify my childhood as perfect, though. One precarious complication bore the influence to turn my dreamy California childhood into an unimaginable nightmare. Leaving me no choice besides facing my darkest fear head-on, day and night. I'm talking about, of course, my wardrobe.

Being a young family, money for frivolous clothes remained out of our reach. This kept the legendary OP shorts and shirts I yearned for on the store's shelf. So despite my lofty position on the school's social pyramid, the clothes I wore sucked my soul dry. Each day equated to slipping on an atrocious costume made from terrestrial leeches, only less fashionable.

Whenever I strutted across the playground, in my mind, I envisioned myself as a displaced hayseed who stumbled into sunny California from the muddy cornfields in Nebraska holding a homemade banjo and chewing on a stick. The only thing my homespun ensemble lacked was a swollen black eye—a nasty shiner from pappy's punch—which I deserved, of course, for oinking at him like a pig when I caught him licking pork fat grease off the kitchen's dirt floor. Again.

But my family's fortunes improved, and my mom surprised me on a random Saturday afternoon. She came into the house carrying a shopping bag from Miller's Outpost, putting my juvenile sense of greed on high alert. And when she tossed the pair of brown OP shorts she bought for me onto the couch, I stumbled around in bouncy disbelief like an astonished contestant on *The Price Is Right* when Rod Roddy's booming voice announces the prize parked behind the vinyl curtain is a brand-new car!

I wore my new shorts at all times. So often, in fact, that in less than a month, I ground the corduroy bands down until the seat of my shorts appeared smoother than the *Star Wars* pillowcase on my bed. I begged for another pair and beamed with ravenous delight when I got them. This pair was light blue, the same color of Superman's bodysuit, which is who I impersonated every time I pulled them on.

On most days after school, my older brother and I walked to a park up the block from our house. We climbed on the jungle gym, rode skateboards, and threw tennis balls for our dog Buffy to fetch.

But the weekends ruled. We loaded up the family Corolla and drove to either Laguna or Aliso Beach. I spent all day on top of a boogie board waiting for the perfect wave, which scrambled me up like an egg if I lost my nerve during the drop and took my hands off the board.

Consequently, I survived two legitimate brushes with death in one day, frolicking in the playful surf instead of focusing on the Pacific Ocean's untold might. But less than twenty minutes after each brief sit-down with the Grim Reaper, I popped up, grabbed my board, and paddled back out for another go.

After watching the sunset, we left the beach, never failing to stop at McDonald's for dinner on our way home. During this time, I developed a primitive craving for a post-beach-day Big Mac, and the sight of those luminous golden arches made my mouth water like Pavlov's dog.

Sure, today legions of crazed nutritionists assert food from McDonald's, if eaten more than once a month, would cause an unsuspecting Russian pooch's tummy to boil over and liquify its critical organs, dead in ten minutes flat. But back in the freewheeling '70s, a freer time when medical doctors encouraged pregnant women to smoke, the sight of the shiny, gold wax paper wrapped around a lamp-heated Big Mac with cheese triggered my primal instincts responsible for the continuance of life.

During the drive, my mind got so locked into the intensity of longing, I started hallucinating fairy tales as a primitive stopgap measure to trick myself into thinking time moved faster. This psychedelic folk tale took place back in the 1800s and centered around an imaginary gold prospector who answered when people asked for Willie B. Rockbottom.

A handsome and unmarried fellow, Willie lived a life of blaring desperation, made much louder when he got fleeced by a stickup gang and lost the rest of his net worth playing midnight blackjack in a bandit's bar outside of Dodge City, Kansas. Days later, sunscorched from crawling down Main Street begging townsfolk for poison, Willie found inspiration at the bottom of a corn whiskey jug and pushed on, empowered by the nonsensical ramblings about gold he overheard in a conversation between a one-legged hooker and the newly rich rascal paying her to hop with nuggets. And so, Willie, demonstrating the measured sensibility of a fruit fly approaching a bin filled with crushed grapes, took his demonic thirst for quick riches and shot out west.

But Willie struggled to find gold. In fact, all he accumulated during his ill-advised treasure hunt comprised of searing pain, irreversible poverty, and a screaming case of chlamydia. Utterly defeated, Willie let the shovel fall from his hands and laid down, accepting his fate as a late lunch for the circling buzzards overhead. But he leaned up and took one last hopeless peek at the brown mound of uneconomical mud in his battered river pan. And instead of seeing another metaphorical pile of the earth's waste, he spotted a fat golden flake shining through the silt, like a rapeseed oil candle flickering up from the floorboards of a boomtown's busiest outhouse. *Eureka!*

I often wondered if Willie B. Rockbottom experienced the same kind of hypnotic joy as me when I caught the first glimpse of the treasured golden arches after a breezy day at the beach, if only for a moment. Until a canyon bandit crept up behind poor Willie, split open the soft part of his skull with a pickax, and scampered off to San Francisco to blow his fortune on clothes designed for a French pimp.

At this point in Willie's rags-to-ditches tale, we pulled into McDonald's, and my ravenous hunger gobbled up any aspirations to fabricate a less realistic conclusion to Mr. Rockbottom's ho-hum life.

Once home, I hopped in the shower to scrub the sand and salt off my body, then climbed into my pajamas and collapsed on the couch, watching movies until I conked out. One of my favorite movies was Neil Simon's *The Goodbye Girl.*

I fell head over heels for Lucy McFadden, the cutest, most beautiful girl on earth. Her unflappable poise left me awestruck.

Throughout the film, I drooled, smitten by the way she traded wily quips with her mom's feisty love interest, Richard Dreyfuss, mailing in a watered-down version of his fast-talking, know-it-all sarcastic, shark-hunting nerd from *Jaws*.

And while her hot-mess mom, a thirtysomething Broadway dancer, continued coming unglued, Lucy McFadden kept her freckled little chin held up high. And since all her displays of courage took place in New York City, my adoration for Lucy compounded out of a definable range. I mean, anybody can put their brave little face on when life goes sideways in Sheboygan or Des Moines. Try Gotham if you want me to care.

My family never vacationed to New York, and I never planned on going, but because of Lucy McFadden, New York City became the only destination I ever circled on a map.

We lived next door to a super cool family. They personified the blowy and eccentric human characteristics famous for generating the sublime energy powering California's grand ambition.

The shaggy-haired man of the house taught photography at the local college and built a specialized darkroom in his garage. He shot and developed subdued collections of award-winning black-and-white photographs of flotsam and various beach-dwelling creatures. Sometimes he showed me portraits of a yawning sea lion or a dramatic long shot in which he captured the elegant confidence radiating off a flock of sedated pelicans gliding over choppy white ocean waters in reverent formation—the cryptic, visual essence of peace, harmony, and flow—or so he said.

His wife sported short, dirty-blond hair and wore flowing dresses, making me think she lived in an elevated state. A passionate English teacher, working in the advanced wing of the high school. They chowed down granola by the bag and exercised as often as dentists brush their teeth. The first health nuts I ever met. Naturally, they spent the bulk of their free time playing in the splendid outdoors. Being avid campers, they utilized their completely rad Toyota Chinook to explore the best parts of the beaches and parks nestled in the most remote and pristine parts of the state. In short, they depicted the consummate diametric version of my midwestern parents.

But we all got along fine in every respect because, I think, each family grew equally enamored with neighborly intrigue about the other. Oh, they also had an exceptional daughter busy setting academic records in high school. She was tall and tan with a sun-streaked blonde mane streaming down to her waist. Gorgeous, more bookish than bombshell, which made her more attractive and likable. She dreamed about becoming a marine biologist and owned all these excellent books about the ocean and whales. I flipped through them with her whenever she babysat on nights our parents went out for dinner.

During this time of my life, the halcyon days of my youth, the upcoming premiere of Carl Sagan's *Cosmos* on PBS was all the rage. America deemed the night *Cosmos* premiered an event. We took part and cohosted a viewing party at our neighbors' house. A few hours before the show started, my dad and our neighbor fired up the grill to cook fish, while the women sautéed vegetables and tossed a healthy salad together in the kitchen.

An ice chest filled with beers sat on the back porch. The beer cooling inside was Henry Weinhard's, well known for being a high-end beer. Months before, I found an empty bottle of the stuff littered on the beach. I picked it up for the trash but paused to study the bottle's arresting label, which displayed a stately golden eagle perched in front of a prominent family crest or a distinguished coat of arms, suggesting the beer bubbling inside should be savored and served during momentous occasions, like toasting a promotion or celebrating nuptials with dear friends at an elegant wedding down in Newport Beach.

These artistic details dug an enduring trench into my brain, and I grew more and more uneasy watching my dad guzzle each one down faster than the last, like a jumpy colt getting nursed by a rural veterinarian.

I counted the number of bottles he drained. Before the show about deep space started, he had already sucked down nine beers with the gravitational pulling capacity of a black hole and showed no signs of slowing down. Keeping a running count guilted me into heating up with shame, as if I were somehow betraying my dad by taking notes. But the way he inhaled our neighbors' exclusive beer, showing no regard for its admirable quality and considerable expense, rattled my sense of fatherly respect.

When my dad drank too much, he got a few notches louder. This never bothered anybody because he was always the funniest guy in the room. He told incredible stories and jokes (with the craft and timing of a young David Brenner), which elevated his humor into a rarefied space.

My dad came hardwired with an exceptional comedic wit and, with no visible effort, turned an ordinary experience about trying to buy dress shoes in Nebraska into a master class on observational monologues. He controlled this spellbinding ability to shift between reasonable practicality and the undue abstract with the uncomplicated aplomb of a Michelin-rated chef preparing a grilled cheese sandwich for a child. His stories provided the shrewd listeners in the room with the elusive answers to life's most burning metaphorical questions. So anytime he launched into a story, I did my best to keep up, hanging on to his every word.

I remembered short clips of my dad when he drank too much and stumbled. These slippery blips made me uncomfortable, sure, but I considered his gaffes sporadic enough to tag as isolated and harmless, like a blurry glitch in the film projecting on a movie screen. Poof. Gone before anyone works up the courage to complain.

But what I witnessed on the night *Cosmos* premiered made me think this glitch on the screen might spark the theater into flames.

The situation regressed once he crossed the point of no return (twelve beers apparently) and started powering down, as if the goblins managing his control board fell asleep on the job or decided, as a goof, to dial his brain waves down until they leveled off to mirror the cerebral activity pattern of a ball-peen hammer or the hosts of the hit show *Real People*.

He mumbled incoherent gibberish throughout an uncomfortable dinner, speaking directly to no one and emitting sounds comparable to a wild boar chewing through a tractor tire.

"Nebraska football. Farm boys throw pigs. Built tanks. No way win war."

He went silent. But the relief of my dad abandoning all efforts to make humanlike sounds with his mouth didn't last because, although quiet, his entire body froze like a petrified rock. The only proof of life came from the visible rage still boiling behind his black eyes, which gazed blankly out into something I hoped to never encounter in waking life or during my worst nightmares.

In what I categorized as an act of divine intervention, *Cosmos* began. We gathered around the television. Alas, my dad did too. He managed to stagger to a recliner and fell into the cushioning with the easygoing grace usually on display when a Kodiak bear gets shot with a high-powered rifle. But minutes before Dr. Carl Sagan started taking us to the edge of the universe aboard his spaceship of the imagination, my dad, thank God, passed out cold.

But soon, he started snoring right in the center of our spooked neighbors' living room, introducing them to his ferocious snore, which worked hard, wheezing air in with more complications than a dying racehorse, using every available muscle to suck in enough oxygen to fill the Goodyear Blimp, to the point an additional molecule would make his chest burst open. After a spine-chilling pause, he returned the air in a jarring series of explosive pops normally heard from a cracked tailpipe.

I had suffered through his snore many times, but never the drunk version. His audible assault on our space intensified until the snore sounded inorganic, more like a tank rumbling through a fishing village after shelling it to smithereens, which made keeping up with Carl Sagan's astronomical projections numbering in the billions and billions impossible.

My sweet mom, who somehow remained calm, eased over and gave my dad a gentle nudge. At this point, I didn't think my dad would twitch if a nuclear bomb exploded in the fireplace. But the second my mom touched him with her tender hand, he jumped like she stabbed him with a steak knife. He acted confused and disoriented, having no idea where he was.

After time stood still for billions and billions of years, he snapped to attention like a soldier. And he zeroed in on my mom. Not looking at her but through her, maintaining a depraved thousand-yard stare. I had never confronted more lifeless eyes, at least on a human. They reminded me of the black pieces I used playing Chinese checkers and might materialize as less unsettling plugged into the hollowed-out eyeball sockets carved into a dead shark's pointed face. And in slow motion, his eyes rolled back.

"Fuck. You. Fuck you. It's all shit. Fuck you!"

Considering the ridiculous number of beers the man drank, the fact each word came out clear and decipherable boggled my mind then and for years afterward. But I couldn't move or breathe. Trapped inside the crumbling house of my reality, now choking on smoke, all my belongings engulfed in the flames created from my dad bombing the only structure I understood back a billion years.

My mind erupted with fear, shame, and rage. All the sturdy wires in my brain responsible for circulating everything I came to believe in and trusted melted down into a lavalike river of copper and thermoplastic hellfire, which continued flooding downward, reducing my anchored reference points about childhood into a charcoal briquette.

Coincidently, about a year later, I experienced a similar bout of emotional trauma seeing *The Empire Strikes Back*—the moment Darth Vader explained to Luke that he'd grown uncomfortable touting himself as the galaxy's most evil man because, at the end of the day, he couldn't stand being a deadbeat dad. He pinged Luke to make amends, eager to patch things up and try parenting on for size.

Come on, Dad. I can't pick up all these leaves!

Use the rake, son. Use the rake.

In any event, not long after the *Cosmos* premiere, I came to realize my dad's soul, or whatever immaterial engine powered the man, had run out of gas. In retrospect, an odd thing to consider at my age. I think any normal kid would've broken down and sobbed or, at a bare minimum, taken their first step toward a thirty-year state of boozy depression.

To be sure, his behavior shook me to the core. But inexplicably, I wanted to save him. First, to attempt connecting in such a way where I understood who the hell he was, or at least used to be. Then figure out how to top his tank off, providing the fuel he needed to travel back to where I needed him most.

Hi there, folks. I'm Skip Stephenson. Welcome to another episode of Real People! *Tonight, we're doing a story about a boy who lives right here in California. His name is Jason Carter. Now he may come off like a normal, all-American kid, but what makes him so unique is his stupidity and this inability to tell the difference between what's possible and what most normal folks would call idiotic gibber-jabber.*

But first, newspaper errors!

HOOK, LINE,
AND DRINKER

Once his physical involvement in the Vietnam War concluded, my dad studied hard and picked up an MBA. He accepted a general manager's role offered by a chemical company on graduation day. And since he never expressed a pip of enthusiasm regarding his career, I figured he treated work the way most adults approached their jobs—with the same chirpy gratitude wired through prison guards probing rectums for contraband.

But not long after the transient astronomical event in which my dad vaporized his world as the rest of us enjoyed *Cosmos*, he received a lucrative offer from a massive, multinational oil company.

I suspected this encapsulated the moment he'd dreamt about since mustering up the courage to decamp from the family farm.

Because, overnight, the two tons of military-grade remorse he had hauled around like a torpid pack mule vanished without a trace, like important luggage at the airport, or leading-man roles for Ned Beatty after the rape scene in *Deliverance*.

This announcement injected me with a transmittable sense of relief. I became so used to my dad reacting the way Bruce Banner does after stubbing his toe, I ignored the temperamental pain chiseling away on my insides.

His promotion came with a hefty raise and a coveted slot on the executive track—with one slight catch. The new position reported out of the corporate office located in Saudi Arabia. Admittedly, my heart sank. Leave California? Sure, when I'm dead. But the contagious way my dad beamed rolled down to me, reducing my geographical concerns down to nothing. I readied myself to follow this version of my dad to the other side of the earth and beyond.

When he explained to my brother and me the academic rigor awaiting us at the renowned private school populated with other kids from all over the world, he couldn't contain his giddy excitement. And once we matriculated into high school, we'd get to pick which one to attend: the one in Paris or the one in London.

I never doubted my dad wanted his two sons a billion light-years away from the small-town stage he walked across on graduation day. And from the overjoyed way he spoke, this opportunity marked the most meaningful moment of his life.

He grew up an only child on a modest farm in a town with three hundred people. And he was the only one in his graduating class of six students brave enough to defy the generational convention of financial well-being afforded to those born into families blessed to own economical plots of nutrient-rich farmland in the Midwest.

Instead, against the reasonable pleas of his parents and friends, he set off for California, searching for his boulder made of gold. I hoped to tell my own kids one day I stood beside my dad when his shovel, at last, cracked open a glowing rock, and we all screamed, "Eureka!"

But once my mom joined the conversation, the story took a hard turn because she promised to throw the total weight of her support behind moving halfway around the world to live in the Middle East as soon as hell froze over.

Looking back, I can appreciate how fast the frail stitching threaded through the tattered fabric of their marriage would've come undone by the additional tug of moving to the other side of the planet. Moreover, this job offer came four months after a group of Iranian college students stormed the US embassy in Tehran and made hostages out of fifty-two Americans. But at the time, from my childish perspective, her outright refusal to consider my dad's dreamy vision came across as shortsighted, if not a mean thing to do.

A few weeks later, my dad took my brother and me on a fishing trip. From the moment his fantasy of becoming an international oil executive got squashed, he went through the motions of life in a dejected trance.

The four-hour drive down the 405 to San Diego on a Friday afternoon during rush hour did little to lighten his gloomy mood.

He booked an overnight tuna run, sailing out from San Diego Harbor. We didn't have to board the boat until 10:00 p.m. So once we arrived in San Diego, having hours to burn, we went to a legendary Italian restaurant in the Gaslamp Quarter to gorge on pizza and spaghetti.

This restaurant introduced me to the old school. Empty green jugs of wine hung from the ceiling, and the tables underneath were covered in red-and-white checkered tablecloths. The family who ran the famous establishment treated us like old friends, pointing out everything on the menu came served after getting whipped together from scratch.

Here, the original seed of contempt for chain restaurants got planted inside my prefrontal cortex, and as I grew older, this seed developed a knack for sprouting up like a plastic flower shot out of a clown's gun anytime I found myself getting dragged into places like Olive Garden or Applebee's.

The thing I loved most about these deep-sea fishing trips was how fast the night temperatures dropped, like a shark hook baited with a go-kart. And before we left, my dad let me dig through his closet and pull out a sweatshirt to wear on the boat. Some of his sweatshirts came from his days in the Marines, but most of them displayed his polarizing affection for Nebraska football. Because they were his, cloaked in either one, I beamed with pride. As if wearing one meant he trusted me enough to rustle through his personal belongings until finding the one I liked.

When the boat left the harbor, we stayed on the deck to scrutinize the Navy's fleet and ogle the sparkling skyline until she faded into blackness, like an alluring actress bowing out of a well-received play, as the fishing vessel pushed farther out to the end of the world.

Afterward, the kids on the boat messed around with the live bait and fiddled with the heavy tackle while the adults sat around the front of the ship chatting about sports and politics as they pounded down beers.

Around one in the morning, most people headed below deck to sleep. The room contained ten bunk beds. My spring-slashed mattress stunk of urine, salt water, and last week's catch. Despite the stench and the nauseating motion of the boat bobbing over the ocean's massive rolling swells, I slept soundly through most of the night.

I woke up once, though, with a jolt, startled by the shrill sound of a familiar snore. My heart stopped beating. If this snore belonged to my dad, I vowed to jump off the boat hugging an anchor. But the mystery man choked himself awake, then started thrashing under his blanket like a gaff-hooked tuna tagged inside a burlap sack. And once I figured out the man dying was a stranger, a nobody, the urge to belt out a joyous, seafaring song to express my euphoric joy grew so strong I bit my lip to keep quiet.

To everyone's relief, the human woodchipper fell back asleep and, I presume, continued living. And for the rest of the night, the only sound came from the boat's rumbling diesel engine.

The captain rang the iron bell to wake us up at six in the morning. When I came up to the deck, I noticed my dad nursing a beer. I remember thinking, *Oh, right, men drink beer at breakfast. But in college, right?*

But before I continued giving this remarkable thought deeper consideration, the boat found itself trolling over a massive school of yellowfin tuna.

We hooked and pulled in too many jumbo-sized fish to count. Each one weighed anywhere from twenty to eighty pounds. When the fish stopped biting late in the day, I couldn't lift my arms high enough to scratch the fish scales and blood off my chin. Having legs as spry as timbered logs, waterskiing behind the boat seemed easier than walking a foot without face-planting on the boat's slippery deck.

I balanced myself and walked toward the bunk room, fueled by the hope of sleeping back to the harbor. But the thought of curling up in a bed used to shoot walrus porn in the off-season replenished my attention. So, I saddled up in a chair at the front of the boat, popped open a Coke, and glued my eyes to the horizon.

After an hour lasting a month, I began counting backward from one hundred, wishing San Diego's skyline popped out of the water each time I finished. After I overheard the ride back takes seven hours, I stopped counting and focused on wishing to be anywhere else on earth.

My dad showed up. I nodded, too tired to wave. He lumbered over to the ice chest, grabbed me another Coke and a fresh beer for himself. On the long ride in, he reached back into the cooler and fished out more beer than I bothered counting.

Two grizzled men came up to the deck from the bunk room and went straight to the cooler.

"Where's all the damn beer?" one of them screamed.

My dad didn't move and stayed quiet. My heart stopped beating and dropped through the bottom of the boat. The men thirsting for beer grew livid, fired up enough to donkey-kick Shamu in the blowhole for splashing their delighted kids during a show. The situation escalated to where the captain inserted himself in the middle of the fray, piping mad and eager to solve the mysterious disappearance of his ship's entire supply of beer.

"It must be a packing mistake," he said.

Then he boasted how his boat never ran out of beer, on overnight trips or otherwise. I cringed, imagining the most shameful conclusion. Mercifully, the predicament ended without bloodshed when a deckhand pulled a bottle of Jim Beam out from the galley, allowing peace to prevail.

My dad stayed silent, doing his best to hold down the boiling acids of a killer hangover while failing to reign in the mobbing remorse corrupting every pickled cell in his body. He looked sad and tired—a haunted portrait of a man lost at sea.

Slowly, he stood up and walked to the stairs leading down to the bunk room, disappearing below without muttering a word. I found an isolated spot on the boat for the remainder of the long, distressing haul to shore.

In a blink, San Diego's magical skyline appeared, triggering a lust bordering on lurid, making me ache with a vexing desire. Then the skyline's beauty melted down into a mist and disappeared. It was gone, ripped out of view, as if the city's image was too much to be processed by a childish brain still incapable of understanding miraculous encounters with blinding magnificence led to crushing disappointment.

I didn't comprehend the shimmering image before my eyes was a cruel mirage, flaunting her impossible attainability and seducing me to believe that selling my soul for the briefest touch exemplified heaven's fairest trade.

These convoluted thoughts amplified my hunger, reminding me how much I loved McDonald's. And, coincidently, I recalled flipping through the pages of a *Playboy* magazine for the first time and encountering Bo Derek's perfect tan and sandy sweet tits.

On the drive home, I chewed through the likelihood my parents' marriage was all but finished. The textured and colorful tapestry of their relationship, woven together with their singular and affecting personal and connected histories, chemically stripped down to molecular mush, and regenerated into construction-grade two-by-fours now sitting on a table saw. And despite it all, they're still fused by the billions and billions of intricate touchpoints proven to exist in the boundless, barely explored galaxies of human intimacy. Still formed as a single being, waiting, listening for the telling click of the saw's switch to slice their intertwined world in half with the ease of lopping a square of butter from a warm stick to spread over a runza roll.

I wondered what my new home would be like once their lives landed on opposite ends of the floor. And for the first time, I applied committed reasoning to the notion anything projecting the capacity to deliver meaningful gratification must be a mirage.

THE SON HARVEST

To the surprise of nobody with a half-functioning brain, my parents got divorced. And while they sorted through the carpenter's dust, they shipped my brother and me to Nebraska, where we weathered phase one of our life's unaccredited reconstruction plan, hanging out on our grandparents' farm.

All things considered, this counterproductive geographical development thrilled me. Because if it didn't lack a ride like Space Mountain and a nightly firework show modeled to make German blitzkriegs resemble humanitarian food drops over Cambodia, their rural farm outside of Palisade (population: three hundred) was no different from my own personal Disneyland.

Their farm accounted for a thousand acres. And everything on it—fields sprouting with giant stalks of corn, rolling hills blanketed with sorghum grass for the cows, an enchanted half acre sectioned off for burning trash—was set against a poetic backdrop of transparent, smog-free skies expanding in every direction with incomprehensible speed toward the black holes Carl Sagan claimed sucked them up, as if they never existed.

My brother and I explored every square inch on the farm. We walked the property carrying rifles or shotguns and took turns taking shots at birds or empty beer cans. A mindless distraction offering a welcome break from my frantic search for clues about my unknown future. The countless piles of fresh cow manure shining under every step I took notwithstanding, naturally.

After raising enough hell, we cooled off in the river running through the heart of their land. Unfortunately, most locals were too spooked to jump in and swim with us because, allegedly, around fifty years back, the town's favorite country bumpkin did multiple backflips off a county bridge to impress the girls and took in a barrel or two of the river's murky water. Soon after, while churning a batch of homemade vanilla ice cream, as happy as a beaver building a twig dam, he dropped dead. The townspeople called it "yellow fever."

And truth be told, this river behaved more like a creek. But since my happy-go-lucky days at the beach got table-sawed into a fading dream, I called this brown-water creek gurgling southward like sludge under a glassy sheen of pesticidal runoff pouring in from surrounding farms a damn river.

The one thing this town did have, though, was a summer base-ball team for kids my age, which, at the time, was the only thing resembling a lifeline. Like a sturdy house stocked with provisions and modest quarters, all built with unwitting drifters like me in mind, desperadoes needing a safe place to regroup after getting flattened by yet another one of life's colossal shitstorms.

This team played for the people, with the town's name, Palisade, stitched with modest pride across the front of each jersey. Lacking anything else to do, the games drew substantial crowds, bringing out the young and old to lap up some baseball and drink iced tea after a long and dusty day, most of which was spent working the fields or on tractors harvesting crops.

Thirty to forty miles in either direction sat four farm towns comparable to ours, with baseball teams of their own. Most of the townspeople traveled in caravans to away games to cheer us on, hauling baskets filled with ham sandwiches and fried chicken to gobble up between plays.

The kids on my team were cool. Cool in the effortless way kids can be when they're confident enough to waddle through life as the most authentic version of themselves. They never swam in the ocean, played tennis, or sat in the stands of a Major League Baseball game. And I never caught one of them sitting on a porch tuning a banjo, picking his teeth with cattle straw.

And yet, I struggled to perceive these boys as something apart from backward-ass hayseeds to the core. Despite my casual attempts to appreciate the simple goodness of their lives,

I presented myself cloaked in urban disdain like the arrogant little prick from California I was. Absurd. Because for all practical purposes, whenever I entered the scene, unquestionably, their story about me revolved around the fact I was pretty much a fatherless bastard without a home to hang my hat on when the sun went down. A harsh but accurate summary of my devolving narrative. Damn those clear-eyed, plainspoken yokels.

The blast crater left from my parents' divorce rocked my foundation but didn't tip me over. Sure, my self-esteem abandoned me, electing to hang back in California, last seen splashing around in the surf with a pigtailed blonde. Teetering, yes, but still standing upright.

In many ways, my mom and dad's split brought sweet relief. My dad's boozy act became a nightly event anchored by the corresponding tenets of a scripted program—predictable in tone, theme, and length. Not unlike Johnny Carson's monologue if *The Tonight Show* broadcasted from hell. Although, anyone who's been to Burbank might argue it was.

The bulky dread I amassed analyzing my dad's next drink—which had grown a billionfold after *Cosmos*, when he mutated into a venom-spewing alien—dispersed like chalk dust before I finished boxing up my bedroom for the move. Who needed Christmas?

The last game of the summer pitted us against the kids from Indianola, Nebraska. This was Palisade's fiercest rival. The long-standing civic friction grated against the existing shrines of economic inequality. As a result, youth baseball games provided the only idealized, universally revered platform for two warring communities to come together as one to spit in the other's face.

By every measure, the town I suited up for was the displaced panhandler in the equation. Indianola maintained a sizable population, administered better schools, and oversaw downtown parades with actual floats rolling past more than one bar. The way I heard it, they pranced around like royalty singing songs satirizing Palisade's distinguished history of bringing diseased crops to market, failing the state's literacy test, and promoting the emotional and economic benefits realized from the aggressive practice of inbreeding.

When our procession pushed into their "metropolis," I admit, compared to my adopted hometown of Palisade, it outshined Cloud City. And seeing the gaping quality of life discrepancies up close ticked me off. But while Indianola boasted every civic, educational, and economic advantage, I set out to prove with conclusive authority that Palisade had the best pitcher on the mound.

And I did, pitching a ferocious game—one of my best, giving up only two runs off five dinky hits, along with ten emasculating strikeouts. After paddling their ass with a cedar plank, being a part of the win, and falling into the town's warm embrace, which dulled my emotional pains like a lidocaine wrap, I was convinced my life was finally primed to start trending up.

After the game, my teammates and I cruised around the ballpark with Cokes, seeing if any of us had the guts to chat up Indianola's good-looking girls. But before finding out, a band of strapping farm boys from their team blocked our path. To which I said something stupid like, "Uh, nice game."

Their country-bred response surprised me. A hard punch to my face, and I got my ass kicked in short order, taking multiple shots to the head and ribs before getting rammed down to the ground like a runaway calf. An adult ran over, breaking the fight up fast, and they scattered faster than foxes fleeing a chicken coop, spooked from the clicking sound of a rifle getting cocked. My teammates stood around me, looking down, unimpressed.

"Why didn't you throw a punch?" one asked.

"I thought I did," I said. A cowardly lie.

When we got back to the farm, for no specific reason, I grabbed one of my grandfather's Winston cigarettes and a pack of matches, then snagged two beers out of the basement refrigerator and soft-stepped out of the house. Dazed, sad, and indeed, thoroughly humiliated, I wandered around the farm, guided by the moon's quieting light. Whatever part of me still pulling away from the black hole sucking me in, I assessed, was already running on fumes.

I walked to the "river," sat down, and cracked open a beer. Then I took a squinted slug, refusing to believe Andre the Giant's crack sweat likely tasted better. I popped a Winston between my lips and held it still for at least a minute, sucking on the smoky paper wrapped around the filter before finally striking a match to light it.

The beer and smoke soothed my brain. I was calm, in control, and processing the world with a more mature, hardened sensibility. When I emptied the first beer, I detected a welcome slack between life's hook hitched through my brain and knotted to an incessantly taut pulling line.

I found being this loose and unburdened by mad and chatty thoughts unusual but otherwise agreeable. Was this how a normal boy my age was supposed to feel?

I pulled the tab down on the second beer, knowing all I could do was guess.

THE DEBASEMENT

I called my nonfarming grandparents, from my mom's side, Nani and Papo. They lived in Omaha and, in the middle of a lasting string of business success, built a sizable, split-level house on a lush acre of woodland perched on a cliff's edge overlooking the whirlpools circulating on top of the Missouri River's deep, southbound flow.

And in the immediate years following their daughter's divorce, we spent regular clusters of time plastering the pieces of our broken lives back together at their home.

Nani embraced her family-centric Czechoslovakian heritage and believed a family gathering for any reason short of a funeral provided an excuse to acknowledge life's blessings. Ever the optimist, her bullish domestic outlook compelled me to keep one hand pressed against the rotting trunk of our storm-dinged family tree.

Together, Nani and Papo assembled into an elegant couple and personified the unfussy class and sophistication of the metropolitan Midwest. I recognized this early in life and used them as a North Star of sorts, always looking to them for guidance on behaving in situations requiring social tact and polish.

Nani appeared in the kitchen early in the morning. Her cheeks rosy with blush, already draped in fashionable clothes and jewelry, delighted to be alive and starting a new day with her coffee and cigarettes. She smoked Merit 100s. And when she leaned into the flame of her silver-plated table lighter to spark one up, I sometimes speculated her to be a long-forgotten but still striking starlet from the heyday of black-and-white films.

Papo fought in the Big One and came home decorated in heroic emblems of war. Once settled, he opened a boutique brokerage firm and made a mountain of money selling civic bonds on behalf of small Nebraska towns short of the cash required to build grain elevators, pave roads, and update school sewage systems to stop exploding on days when the cafeteria served chili for lunch.

On a wall in their entertainment room hung a framed picture of Papo and his firm's partners—a hand-drawn sketch, one of those black-and-white caricatures wandering artists draw at amusement parks or county fairs for a quarter. The cartoon picture exaggerated his handsome features and inflated the size of the cigar in his hand to mimic a Navy ship's torpedo.

In most cartoonish depictions of humans, the unwitting subject's worst features are passive-aggressively celebrated by the shifty crackpot doing the sketch. But this picture managed to capture and amplify all the intelligence and warmth purring behind his shimmering blue eyes the same way the five-hundred-cubic-inch engine under the hood of his Cadillac idled at a red light.

He retired long before we started showing up but still greeted each day with a fresh shave, wearing a crisp white shirt, pressed wool slacks, and one of his distinguished wristwatches, always polished and shining like a nugget of gold.

When we stayed at their house, we dressed up on Saturday nights to go out for fancy steak dinners. They picked up a snappy three-piece suit for me from Petersen Harned Von Maur at Westroads Mall. Slipping the suit on boosted my flagging esteem. When I buttoned up the jacket in front of a mirror, I might've confused myself for a child star more than once.

Papo drove us to Mister C's Steak House or the Omaha Club in his newest Cadillac. A car I came to believe General Motors designed with him in mind. The same way an Italian shoemaker handcrafts a pair of leather dress shoes to convey his respect to a man he admires.

Omaha got soaked with rain often. I welcomed how the wipers on Papo's Cadillac didn't make a sound swishing back and forth, pushing buckets of rain off the windshield to make driving safe enough to keep moving forward. An appropriate mechanical nod to how they lived their lives, a collaborative manifestation rooted in refined strength and galvanized by protective purpose. I felt more comfortable and safe riding in the back of his car than a duckling dreaming in a nest made of silky feathers plucked from the plump flank belonging to Mother Goose.

Symbolically speaking, when rain caused my mom to engage the wipers of our Corolla, a runaway caged underneath a serial killer's kitchen floor might think their captor was edging two cleavers against the grain of their roommate's skeletonized left femur.

On most nights, Nani and Papo enjoyed two cocktails apiece. A leisurely and noble way to wrap the ribbon around the gift of another pleasant day. I loved mixing up their drinks. J&B Scotch for Papo and Stolichnaya Vodka for Nani, both blended with club soda.

They collected drink stirrers from famous places they dined, like the 21 Club in New York and the ballroom at Caesar's Palace in Las Vegas. After stirring their drinks, I put the stick in my mouth for a bitter taste before tossing the spirited keepsake into a cup filled with warm, soapy water.

It didn't go unnoticed they never drank more than two cocktails and always remained the same, familiar people I grew to love and trust. Considering the way my dad drank (attacking every drop, never stopping, and sometimes turning into Jack Torrance), Nani and Papo presented me with an alternative user's manual for drinking, and I decided, when the time came, to crack it open for a quick read.

During a visit near the end of summer before enrolling in sixth grade, my brother suggested the idea of drinking a lot of booze to better understand the condition scientists refer to as "plastered."

By lucky chance, their house had a basement. And unlike most basements in the Midwest or otherwise, they designed their underground space for reasons having little to do with surviving a nuclear blast or being a safe place to do unimaginable things to shade-tolerant houseplants.

This underground space echoed the part of a cruise ship's deck designated for drinking sunset cocktails. Spacious enough for fifty people to eat, drink, and dance. The sleek Carrara marble floor maintained a permanent shine. And they hired a handyman to paint shuffleboard targets on either side—a sporting, if not benevolent, touch.

But the best thing in their basement was the pool table. Unlike the shoddy pool tables lined up in bowling alleys covered with cigar ash and questionable stains, the sturdy and elaborate construction of their table honored the King's game. They bought it back in the '60s, when America's obsession with billiards flashed into a boiling point the second every man in America questioned his sexuality upon seeing Paul Newman chalk his stick in *The Hustler*.

The basement also had a massive fireplace capable of burning six logs at once. But for our experiment, we turned our attention to the basement's full-sized wet bar, stocked with an unlimited supply of top-shelf liquor. A sign behind the bar read, "Have fun. It's later than you think."

The next school door my brother would pass through granted entry into the uncharted wastelands of high school. Long recognized as a gifted student, he postulated getting bombed to develop a tolerance for booze would help him fit in with the more rowdy and popular kids. I found no reason to question his plan. As a matter of fact, his thinking made more sense to me than directions for cooking instant oatmeal.

But in spirit, I didn't buy in. The idea of getting drunk for no reason seemed silly. I wanted to play Atari or shoot pool. But I never refused a coveted invitation from my older brother to join in on whatever he had in mind. So while he pulled bottles of liquor off the shelf, I yanked a cold Budweiser from the fridge and snapped it open.

Of course, as a soon-to-be man of the sixth grade, I felt comfortable drinking beer, well trained to withstand the rotten flavor until the arousing mission of nominal intoxication was achieved. My battle plan called for taking my sweet time and savoring the moment, influenced by the leadership and teachings of Nani and Papo.

On the other side of the bar, as if taking his cue from "The Plate Spinning Song," my brother started throwing back shots at a breathless clip—rum mixed with scotch, scotch mixed with gin, gin mixed with green syrup—and slugging them down like water, as if his larynx was ablaze in flames.

I enjoyed the show, sipping at my beer while thinking he might measure an inch too short for this adult ride. Mixing liquor? Drinking the stuff straight? Trying to break the *Guinness Book of World Records* entry for glass-to-mouth speed? I thought we were learning how to handle our liquor, but like magic, my studious, even-handed brother vanished in a bursting cloud of stage smoke, replaced by a gyrating monkey on roller skates trying to hump a hole through a bar of soap.

Years later, this dubious moment came roaring back to life thanks to the movie *Cocktail*. But in less time than Bryan Brown's role in *Cocktail* destroyed his reputation as an actor's actor, my older brother streaked a billion light-years past being plastered. He laughed and stumbled around and slurred heady statements like, "Dis is blostum!"

But soon, my brother's rocket ship crashed, and he started hacking his guts all over the place with admirable force, like his mouth was the end of an industrial tube used to drain King Kong's septic tank.

He barfed all night. I stayed up with him and provided my best version of care, checking on him, bringing him water and periodically holding a mirror in front of his nose to make sure he could fog it. With no experience as a Betty Ford nurse, I ran out of ideas and rode out the rest of the night numb with fear. Not unlike a rookie nurse coming unzipped tending to Charlie Sheen on her first shift at Cedars-Sinai.

What upset me the most, I figured out later, was learning my older brother couldn't hold his liquor, and how he failed to remain who he was because of booze. This event thrust me into being my own older brother of sorts, which I hated. I never aspired to this role or had reason to think the part was mine to play.

But these were the cards held in my hands. I drank alcohol like a reasonable man, with control and an easy-breezy demeanor—the same elegant and practiced way Nani and Papo drank this mysterious stuff. Once we left their home, the only example for me to follow would be my own.

After reconciling his experience, my brother never drank more than two cocktails in one sitting ever again. Meaning, unlike most humans, he figured out drinking's binary code with the same evolutionary edification roller-skating monkeys exhibit when soap milled to a clean a bartender's hands rejects their depraved advances.

During this choppy time, I sourced motivation from one place: my fear of pain. As a result, I continued tinkering with the standard two-drink formula in my single-minded quest to enhance alcohol's protective effects, forever fiddling with the metrics to support the ever-changing hypothetical proposition of what constitutes the perfect amount of liquid support needed to cover me dashing from point A to B.

Naturally, I treated this exploration as consequential business, employing the same trusted components of the scientific method utilized by medicine men during the Stone Age in their quest to cure things like dry mouth, headaches, and inflamed genitalia.

CALIFORNIA'S COOLER

When seventh grade rolled around, I lived in Fort Worth, Texas, and had been for two years. And I woke up each day more stumped about my mom getting remarried less than a year after a court clerk stamped and filed the divorce papers before dragging me down to Texas.

To be sure, I liked my new stepdad. Considering most wedding gifts for men are returned for cash or tossed in the banquet hall trash, the fact he did neither to me, in my mind, made him a saint.

Not long after settling in, I redoubled the efforts to shield my emotional contact points from the blinding heat scorching every square inch of where my life took place. I pined for the crisp California climate and missed having a best friend. And thanks to the absence of connected technologies, long-distance calls cost fifty dollars a second. So, for all I knew, my best friend in California may have dropped dead.

To find relatable context associated to my situation, I studied movies about kids my age getting sucker punched by life. Of course, in Hollywood, the best cure came when kids cracked open and prattled about all the neurotic sludge bubbling out from their mangled brains. Timothy Hutton did this with the ruffled but winsome Judd Hirsch in *Ordinary People*. Not only did therapy work, but he also won an Oscar for his dramatic leap of faith.

But here in the real world, the unflinching emotional wasteland of Texas, the family courts treated the outward processing of a divorce as a hanging offense. In fairness to people trying to save lives plying in the black magic of psychology, I lacked the resources to seek out information explaining why my feelings ran amok, the way kids coming unhinged nowadays can acquire principled advice readily available on apps like TikTok and Snapchat from the comfort of their favorite chair or while bawling in the tub.

Actually, the school nurse compiled an obligatory stack of pamphlets to offer kids tumbling down the world's trash chute. But whoever wrote the handouts believed when a family's machinery falls apart like the transmission on a Yugo, the only proven cure is a heaping bowl of Blue Bell ice cream.

In a dysfunctional twist, I found comfort wandering through

life having more questions than answers. Curiosity kept me alert and sharp. And attempting to outwit life's scraggy riddles made time on earth move a little faster, leading me to think I grasped how the world worked better than most kids, wigging or not. But if remaining extra inquisitive about human folly induced a second-rate, homespun buzz, my new interest in girls triggered a staggering, mind-altering high.

A cute and popular girl in my grade hosted a birthday party at her house. About fourteen kids showed up. An equal mix of dumb-struck boys and nail-biting girls. And thanks to raging hormones, making each kid at the party more ashamed by their puberty-ravaged appearance than the entire regional cast of Cats (only a thousand times hornier), a formidable cloud of toxic apprehension emerged, which made breathing impossible.

Of course, this was the '80s, meaning the parents did the responsible thing and went barhopping, abandoning us like an unwanted herd of frisky barn rabbits to fend for ourselves.

Too petrified to speak, we played tapes by Bon Jovi, Duran Duran, and the mind-blowing DJs Run-DMC. The loud music helped weaken the grip squeezing all the life out of the anxious gathering, freeing us to talk in the familiar way we spoke at school. A welcome shift from leering at each other in perverted silence like lewd strangers at the bus station downtown, bargaining in the trade of dirty favors.

As normalcy sluggishly established itself, "Open Arms" by Journey came on. Naturally, the throbbing ballad snapped everyone into a dreamlike, vegetative state, compelling us to pair up and try slow dancing on for size.

If only environmental engineers could've been on hand to convert the sexual tension into a renewable source of clean energy. In that scenario, today, bovine gas would be the biggest threat to global warming, and the tap water in Flint, Michigan, would be renowned for its healing effects on hysterical babies getting dunked in it during baptisms.

When the song climaxed, and with the denim in my Levi's stretched to a ripping point, someone proposed the tempering idea of sitting in a circle to play spin the bottle.

I carried a major-league crush on a girl attending the party—the hottest girl in school by a long shot, not to mention whip smart. I adored her sense of humor too, tracking closer to *Night Court* than *Mr. Belvedere*. The perfect girl. In the spirit of anonymity and, of course, respect, I'll refer to her as Penelope Pillowtits.

The gods of futility blessed me with the game's first spin. Besides switching lives with Ricky Schroder, I never wished harder for anything than the bottle I spun to stop on her. But when the bottle stopped spinning, Bruce Lee may as well have punched a hole through my chest, removed my still-beating heart, and rammed the bloody organ in my mouth, which hung open, slack with shock. Because the bottle, mocking me, came to rest pointed at the girl sitting right beside her.

To be clear, this girl was exceptionally kind, bright, and cute as a button by anyone's measure. As a matter of fact, I liked her plenty—as a friend. But now she sat stooped on the floor, waiting for me to lay one on her. Of course, I had no way of knowing what she thought about the bottle being pointed, unintentionally, straight at her privates. Although, earlier in the school year, we teamed up as lab partners, and when we crossed hands dissecting a dead frog, we didn't pause. And her eyes didn't turn into red cartoon hearts and pop out of their sockets, making me think she thought the same pleasant but decidedly neutral things about me.

So with everyone giggling and ogling, the two of us had to suck face. We both stood up and made our way to the inner circle with our arms reaching out to each other in a mechanical, listless way, as if we were both blind and searching for the handle attached to a bathroom door.

Once we bumped into each other, we leaned into an open-mouth kiss so jilted and sloppy, for weeks after, I fantasized about living in Nepal as a celibate monk. And it's possible she realized her natural sexual orientation during our kiss because years later, after graduating from college with a degree in visual arts, I heard she came out—news that didn't surprise me as much as it made me happy for her.

The next boy to spin was the class goof. He reminded me of the kooky, throwaway characters Disney inserted into cartoon movies to give the line-dancing-biscuits-and-gravy crowd a relatable surrogate to follow and keep them from getting lost in the complicated plots. *Der, uh, Mickey, where we goin' now?*

I believe he "suffered" from what's now called ADHD, which is treated with formidable, highly addictive narcotics made easier to acquire for a child in need today than a box of crayons.

He talked nonstop and never stopped sweating. Anytime he showed up, no matter when or where, he was gassed and drenched in funky perspiration like he just punched his timecard after pulling a double shift at the town quarry.

I didn't dislike him. He was an athlete too, and we played on the same teams and got along fine. And I suppose if someone hosed him down, caulked up his sweat glands, and sprinkled crushed Valium into his morning bowl of Froot Loops, a more profound friendship might've developed.

He gave the bottle a hard spin with his sweaty hands, which got stopped after one rotation by the court-marked edge of a K-Swiss shoe. Seeing the resting bottle pointed at Penelope, my dream girl, I swallowed back a reflexive barf.

Somehow, he made the simple act of standing up seem impossible, struggling to his feet as if the Safari-grade tranquilizer dart his mom stabbed him with before the party started thinning out. Imagine Don Knotts squat-thrusting a freight container filled with canned soup.

He staggered to her, almost knocking her over, like an ape lurching at a crate of fresh bananas. Now, watching Penelope's innocence drown in the ruttish slobber flooding out from an adolescent beast, a human still convinced history's funniest joke revolves around tricking strangers into pulling his finger, was, to say the least, challenging. But seeing her body crumble under the force of insatiable want, no different from a common whore, made the most searing pain I experienced up to this point feel like my toes getting nibbled on by a puppy.

Decades later, while watching *The Ice Storm*, I recognized the pounding torment I experienced that night. In the movie's brilliant key party scene, Kevin Kline's character, a likable fellow, is slumped on the floor, drunk. Minutes later, he's reduced to nonexistence when he's forced to watch the woman he lusts for (the ageless and radiant Sigourney Weaver) pick the keys belonging to a strapping young buck—a clean-cut, much younger man. He glistens with red-blooded vigor and appears better equipped than the Brazilian soccer team to the task of pounding her hot-to-trot body into a smoldering pile of sexual dust.

Later during the party, as my misguided and melodramatic ideas about love continued tumbling downward in the darkness of an infinite, teenybopper abyss, I came upon multiple packs of orange-flavored California Coolers stacked side by side in an old refrigerator kept running in the garage.

And as if provoked by the icebox's interior light, the measured behaviors I took pride in demonstrating whenever I drank fell out of style quicker than Reaganomics and Jordache jeans. I pronounced moderation as passé, if not a hapless show of frumpy cowardliness.

So, I twisted the cap off a bottle and inhaled the contents like a man dying of thirst. The liquid was sharp and fizzy and produced a unique flavor, the way Tang might taste if mixed with paint thinner. But seconds after I choked the whole bottle down, I opened another, drinking this one twice as fast.

In a brilliant orange blast, the dim lights in my mind's shadowy rooms exploded into magnificent hellfire, blinding me with a shine brighter than military searchlights used to spot bombers flying through night skies during a war.

This commanding light healed my broken heart, which started thumping with the power and cadence of a lion devouring a wildebeest after a two-mile chase. I guzzled down another.

Was this fizzy dreck the secret weapon I sought? Or more of a partner? Like an assertive, well-armed ally constitutionally bound to crack back my aggressors? Soon, I thought, we could rule the world. And the more I drank, the easier this decree became to swallow as a hardwired fact.

But as I gauged the scope of my new partnership's destructive reach, I uncovered a potential hitch, the insufficient supply of ammunition. In quiet fear, I froze. What will I do when the wine is gone? I got twitchy and suspicious watching my friends drink through my supply without a thought for fun.

When I opened the fridge and only found a gallon of milk and an unopened gift box from Hickory Farms, I stood frozen with disbelief, horrified, like a statue made of wax. My booze was all gone. In a piercing flash, all my world-beating confidence melted down, the same way Major Arnold Toht's face dissolved at the end of *Raiders of the Lost Ark* when Belloq opened the ark. It's a wonder

I didn't drop to my knees and reach for the sky. *Noooooooooooo!*

Or, Christ, did I?

I woke up the next day in my bed, having no idea how or when I got home. The night didn't go as planned. Then again, no Penelope, no memory, no problem. If this was my first movie about getting blackout drunk, sure, it bombed. But I studied and understood movies. And anyone familiar with the inner workings of Hollywood knows sequels are where the real magic happens and are always a billion times better than the original.

MIGHT AS
WELL JUMP

B efore discovering Warren Zevon's *Excitable Boy* and *Me Against the World* by Tupac Shakur, *Diver Down* by Van Halen topped my list of the greatest albums ever made. I didn't connect with Van Halen right away. I recognized their songs on the radio ("Runnin' with the Devil," "Jaimie's Cryin'," etc.), but their stuff didn't dazzle me enough to add an album or two to my treasured and rapidly growing collection of cassette tapes.

This was more of a clerical issue, having nothing to do with their talent or the negligible amount of my weekly allowance. Especially since, where music was concerned, money was no problem. That's because in the early '80s, cassette tapes cost a good deal less than stamps.

You might remember all any idiot had to do was make up a phony name (John Smith, Stan Smith, or Eaton Beaver) and fill out the Columbia Records promotional flyer folded into every Sunday paper. Then, if you could manage to round up a penny and attach it to the back of this form with Scotch tape, the cocaine-snorting executive kooks running Columbia Records into Chapter 11 heedlessly shipped eight brand-new cassettes of your choosing right to your front door for the cost of postage plus one cent—no joke.

I knew it was too good to be true. Either an economic glitch or a straight-up scam. I suspected a reckless offer like this came with grisly consequences, like an endgame worse than whatever happens to gamblers who burned through a bankroll of cash fronted by the Russian mob.

As a matter of fact, my first encounter with the glossy promotion unsettled me. It looked like a one-way ticket to hell. Even so, I scrambled to sign up, exercising minimal caution.

With my family in the room, I slid the brochure out from the newspaper's fold, tucked it in my shirt, and darted to my room. Once there, I perspired with disgrace, like a petty thief after snatching an old lady's purse from her lap while she catnapped on the crosstown bus. But the lewd anticipation of examining my ill-gotten goods empowered me to brush aside any concerns linked to burning in hell.

Besides, Columbia employed the same influential visual trickery tobacco conglomerates exploited to trigger cigarette cravings in elementary school children by carpet-bombing playgrounds with their irresistibly designed packs of sweet-smelling smokes to hook in new customers. So, really, I had no choice other than to try it.

As I gazed at all the beautiful album covers, like any good little smoker, I lost control over the amount of drool coming out of my slack mouth while vowing to do whatever it took to get my mitts on them.

I used a black pen to check the boxes next to albums of bands I knew and liked or ones with flashy covers that caught my eye. This "first hit is free" style of capitalism hooked me on Ozzy Osbourne, Judas Priest, and Iron Maiden. I also took chances on random bands for no reason besides the one-cent asking price. Why else would a kid my age take chances on albums by Men at Work, The J. Geils Band, and in the spirit of full disclosure, the inspiring genius of Billy Joel?

Another time on another order, and down to my final selection, I checked the box next to the red-and-white album cover fronting *Diver Down* because I reasoned (flush with house money) bands who liked scuba diving must be good.

The package of cassettes took an aggravating eight weeks to arrive. And the second they did, the quick and suspicious way I swiped the box off the front porch would've made anyone nosing around think the package contained porno mags or dope. So then, like a hangdog creep, I smuggled the box into my room and waited for my parents to scram before ripping into the illicit stash.

I rocked out to new albums by Ozzy Osbourne and Mötley Crüe, listening to each compilation in its entirety at full blast no less than three times before slicing into the plastic wrapped around *Diver Down* and cramming their tape into my Walkman.

They played workmanlike, tightly layered music. Nothing blew my hair back. The instrumental "Cathedral" delivered a unique setup to a serviceable remake of "(Oh) Pretty Woman." Intrigued but unimpressed, I listened to the next side. And around the time Eddie's acoustic strumming at the beginning of "Little Guitars" gave way to the tight drum action kicking off the song's next verse, I forgot about every other band on the planet.

I fast-pedaled my bike to the grocery store and bought heavy metal magazines like *Creem* and *Circus*, devouring pages detailing the band and keeping fans abreast of the wanton horseplay taking place during their latest over-the-top live show. And with the steady hand of a surgeon slicing out an arachnoid cyst, I cut out the band's photos, mindful not to botch the article's inspirational copy, and taped Van Halen's rollicking portraits over every square inch of my bedroom walls.

I got my friends to start mainlining Van Halen too. We met up after school and lip-synched songs from the album in my backyard from start to finish like we were playing to a sold-out crowd of hysterical and willing women. I took on the role of David Lee Roth, the cocksure lead singer. I did air splits and herkie jumps the same way he flew and bounced across the stage, as evidenced by the glossy snapshots wallpapering my room.

We tried taking our act on the road and auditioned for the school's talent show. My friends and I took over the auditorium stage, strutting out in makeshift costumes our girlfriends stitched together after almost agreeing to let them apply makeup to our faces.

We chose the song "Dancing in the Streets" and blew the roof off the school, or so I thought. But the fate of our pooled destiny to become rock gods became immediately legible on the pale and disapproving faces of the three frumpy teachers judging the tryouts. Flustered, angry, and disgusted, as if they each took a bite out of the same rotten apple, they didn't allow us to perform and banned us from the show.

But this minor setback didn't stop me from rocking out to Van Halen at all times. Soon, I rounded up another penny and ordered their earlier tapes and listened to nothing else on long road trips or in my room. I scribbled the band's name across the cover and pages inside my schoolbooks instead of reading them for homework, arrested in a daze.

Their music made me forget everything I invested my emotional currency into and shared the same reflexive qualities and characteristics found in unlisted Canadian penny stocks. Meaning whenever business boomed, a breathtaking correction soon followed, leading whatever being or object I trusted with my heart and soul to plunge downward at supersonic speeds. Comparable to John Candy's descent to the bottom of Lake Louise if he dove in to chase down a sinking barrel of craft maple syrup.

And when the news broke confirming Van Halen's new tour, complete with concert dates to promote their latest album 1984, my life's value (no surprise) shot up like a shifty drilling outfit touting tar sand sweet spots outside Alberta.

I counted the days down to the concert, crossing out the squares in a *Sports Illustrated* swimsuit pinup calendar hanging on my wall. Before my alarm buzzed, I popped out of bed each morning and marked the day right away, feeling more excited than I ever did when updating the Advent calendar to track the birth of Jesus Christ.

The night before tickets went on sale, my mom drove me to Dallas at three in the morning to wait in line with a million other desperate fanatics hoping to score tickets to a show expected to sell out in less than a minute.

To outwit the crushing demand, the concert promoters set up a sophisticated lottery system. They passed out plastic wristbands stamped with a number. If they called your number, you got a place in line to buy tickets. If they didn't call your number, your wristband or any piece of foldable trash on the ground could be exchanged onsite for a New Coke or the following week for a front-row seat to see Hall & Oates.

Around the same time, my friends and I were experiencing developmental breakthroughs on the baseball field. Professional ballplayers talk about the peculiar ebbs and flows of the game, its spiritual connection to the past, and the cryptic attributes God must see wired through a man's soul before blessing him with the ability to hit a Major League curveball.

And the only way to grasp a micro understanding of these ethereal concepts happened if the game itself slowed down, in a poetic sense, which happened to a lucky few of us throughout the season. We started swinging our bats with trusted aggression. The balls we threw hissed, and when they found the back of a glove, they clapped like a wooden paddle smacking a boy's bare ass. And when the signal came in from the third-base coach, each of us knew how to lay down a cottony soft bunt to advance a runner, knowing the baseball's spiritual architects had exactly this response in mind when they dreamed up the beautiful game.

Before the all-star season got underway, everyone involved in the league, including the paint-huffing schizophrenic charged with mowing our field's grass, agreed we were an exceptional team wired with the right stuff to go deep in the state tournament and beyond. This was our time.

Throughout my life, I never understood what sequence of events transpire inside the neural pathways interconnected through a man's brain if, while minding his own ordinary business, Dolph Lundgren appears out of thin air and brass-knuckle-punches him square in the nuts. Although the day our all-star team's schedule was posted, recognizing the timing conflict between our first game and Van Halen's concert gave me a clear idea.

In a batty panic, I held up the night of our opening game against the date of Van Halen's show. The date was the same. Again. I double-checked the calendar a thousand more times until—with my own crestfallen balls lodged in the back of my throat, as if Dolph Lundgren had, in fact, followed me home and given them a swift punch—I started crying like a smacked baby.

In sports, rules dictate reason. Without them, sports wouldn't exist. These specific and binding codes set guidelines, define victory, and protect conflicting participants from otherwise killing each other. Throughout history, covering every imaginable culture and sport from American football to Siberian face slapping, millions of rules have been implemented and debated, and continue evolving to keep up with changing times. But above all, I believe these rules provide the one and only concerted layer of governance safeguarding the world from falling into cannibalistic chaos.

For me, the heart of the matter sprang up in the explicit absence of an edict permitting an able-bodied player to skip a game for reasons apart from death. Because throughout human history, the laughable/nihilistic idea an athlete not raised by the devil would opt out of a game for any reason besides death had never been considered, much less discussed. Not as a joke or used as a hokey icebreaker before a keynote speech about the importance of rules. Bailing on my team to bang my head with Van Halen, I understood, would be the equivalent of committing athletic suicide.

But at the same time, I had to admit these dogmatic rules, written centuries before the fundamental inclination in humans to seek out and engage in more meaningful activities fully evolved, needed mending. What about the dedicated athletes also pursuing academic achievement, empowering the spread of humanitarianism, or having the decency to show up when their mistress gives birth to their child? Don't commendable demonstrations of heroism deserve at least one free pass?

Knowing the fair parameters of sport-promoted freedom around the world, I decided to introduce a future-oriented bill to modernize the rules of engagement, clearing the path for all humans to play the game *and* save the world, unburdened by the limiting fears associated with missing a single contest. Besides, our first game pitted us against the worst team in the tournament, a grab bag of uncoordinated but likable nerds who'd prefer to be trading *Star Wars* cards at space camp.

If our team played defense with bare hands and used plastic straws for bats, stomping these dorks down a mudhole would still require less effort than anyone on our team ever expended adjusting their cup. I was humble enough to acknowledge the lack of my participation in the foolproof beatdown would go unnoticed.

Furthermore, wouldn't my absence benefit the team down the road? If I took the night off to rest my golden arm while they blasted every ball Team NASA soft-tossed to Mars, I'd return to the team at full strength for the critical games. Right? I mean, my thinking harmonized with the affecting lyrics of smart baseball's most sacred hymns.

I spent the rest of the night fine-tuning my amendment so that when I introduced the new bill to my parents and coaches the next day, not only would they understand its logic but marvel at how the world survived this long without its widespread application.

But the next day, to my skeptical astonishment, my parents and coaches blew me and my culturally bullish speech off. Instead, they informed me everything would be okay, and the only things on trial were my guiding principles and integrity. So, brilliantly, they put every metric ton of the verdict's oppressive backlash on top of my rickety consciousness. What's a boy to do?

In the end, to be quite honest, I ranked the Van Halen concert as the three best hours of my life. David Lee Roth flew all over the stage. Eddie melted every face in the crowd with his red-and-white striped guitar. And, more shocking, Alex Van Halen and Michael Anthony, the band's two weak links in possession of, at best, garage band talent, behaved in the manner of gods.

Of course, I huffed in a metric ton of secondhand pot smoke during the show, and I'll never be sure if I experienced a contact high, but if the Little League of America conducted drug tests, I might've needed a trainer from the East German Olympic squad to help me pass.

But as the best night of my life went on, stoned or not, an escalating sense of all-consuming paranoia forced me to think of nothing else besides the dishonor associated with bailing on my team. The next day, when somebody asked me what song Van Halen played for their encore, having no recollection of it spooked me.

Over the next two weeks, our team got hotter and steamrolled its way into the Texas state tournament. This was a huge deal, the only topic people talked about—our team picture splashed across the front of the city paper's sports page. And since I had nothing to do with our storied run, all the attention and high praise killed me.

The coaches who used to love me treated me like a cup full of dip spit. When they communicated information to me, they used their hands, primarily gesturing me toward the end of the bench. The same place I sat ever since Van Halen split town on a chartered jet filled with a gaggle of loose groupies and garbage bags stuffed full of high-powered blow.

I didn't whine or pace back and forth in the dugout mumbling like a homeless schizophrenic about an international conspiracy to rid the world of fairness and logic. Instead, I committed to staying positive and kept myself ready for action in the event my number got called. But my upbeat attitude became harder to maintain as we kept winning, with me nailed to the end of the dugout's pine, which might as well have been a sacrificial cross.

For kids caged in the dugout with no hope for parole, clocks stop ticking the same way time stands still for men serving on death row. The suspension of time is a dangerous phenomenon experienced only by those doomed and too stubborn or stupid to understand all hope is long gone. With no way to time-stamp forward motion toward life's bleak conclusion, people like me tend to dive headfirst into infinite loops of dark reflection. Without the regulating ticktocks of a clock to snap people back to earth, these destructive thoughts go on forever, like Keith Richards's buzz, only it's not awesome.

As my teammates turned impossible double plays or hit moonshots out of the park, I obsessed over the cryptic events leading me to triple-flush my baseball career down the toilet. As if all the perfect game added up to became less valuable to me than the unsinkable remains swirling atop the murky water in a truck stop toilet.

I rode the bench all the way to Waco, Texas, home of the Little League state championship. A caravan of friends and family traveled to cheer us on through the games, most of whom took time off from work and planned on treating their week in Waco (provided we kept winning) as a summer vacation.

Our first game was against an advanced team from Brownsville, Texas. I say advanced not because they possessed exceptional skillsets but because their starting pitcher had a beard.

To be sure, his beard lacked the conviction and confidence Robert Redford's beard embodied in *Jeremiah Johnson*. Instead, this "kid's" nappy beard looked like the independent clusters of prickly black whiskers on his face tried to join forces but stopped, gathering in a disagreeable standoff. As a result, the hair splotched across his face likened to a strung-out drifter or the bewhiskered woman squatting in a kissing booth at an unlicensed county fair.

In either case, the fact their team's pitcher had a beard alarmed us enough. To loosen the tense pregame mood, I remarked he must've driven himself to the ballpark in a stolen Trans Am. If the resulting chuckles in the dugout indicated a newfound sense of calm, our confidence remained intact. But once he threw his first warm-up pitch and we heard the umpire scream, "God damn!"

our winning attitude went missing like the pitcher's only can of shaving cream.

In the bottom of the last inning, Brownsville was up 2–0. And if not for a few miracles on defense, the game could've easily been a 10–0 blowout. The only time we got a bat on the ball occurred when our best hitter foul-tipped a changeup into the dirt.

The traveling fans supporting us started packing up before the bottom half of the last inning started. As dejected as gamblers at the track when the horse they bet pooled mob money on snapped a leg rounding the first turn.

Most of the dads stared at the ground, shell-shocked and biting down on cigarettes, acting more like they were at a college buddy's funeral and were reluctant to start covering his casket with ceremonial dirt.

The mood in the dugout was worse. Without speaking, we all agreed our last at-bat was a humiliating formality to denote our all-star dream season's dispiriting conclusion. And in a stunning turn, the coach who had benched me all summer told me to grab a bat—a heartless move more degrading than surprising. Since I batted sixth, the bearded pitcher had a better chance of getting mistaken for the Gerber baby than I had of making my way to the plate before we burned through our three outs.

Three up, three down, as it had been all day. Nobody understood this mathematical certainty more than our coach, and I had no misconceptions he forced me to grab a bat to rub his last handful of spiteful salt into my gaping psychological wounds.

Our first two batters struck out on six straight pitches. And since they both thrashed at the ball with the athletic grace of a blind man fighting off wasps with a broomstick, all hope of a miraculous comeback died on the pine.

But we got a hit. And another. Now we had runners on first and second base, and I stood on deck, petrified with disbelief. In a cryptic turn of events, the bearded pitcher did the unthinkable and threw four balls in a row.

So, with two outs and the bases loaded, I, the reviled Van Halen groupie, came creeping to the plate. The walk to the batter's box took ten thousand years, like I woke up in a prehistoric cave, frozen to the core, struggling now to trudge home, back to my simple hunting village, as my stiff and disgusting hairy body thawed like a bag of freezer meat lodged between a radiator and a brick wall.

I couldn't focus on anything beyond my numb hands gripping the bat. My heart ballooned and pressed through my ribs, clapping faster than a lab monkey participating in an unsanctioned histamine trial. An insurmountable amount of time had passed since I'd faced a live pitcher. So, visualizing the savage lashing awaiting me didn't tax my imagination any more than picturing a ball of brown yarn getting pawed by a cat.

My walk to the plate had nothing to do with baseball. This was a public execution. The rotten little metalhead who ditched his team to rock out with Van Halen would be regarded, forever, as the selfish loser who struck out to ruin everyone's magical season. My friends (and their parents) would hate me forever, and I thought of no reason to fault them for doing so. The batter's box might as well have been a guillotine.

Visually, I didn't make out the first pitch but still swung at an invisible startling hiss, and hard enough to lose my footing and topple over like a sniper shot me in the gut. The parents in the stands groaned, muffling my name attached to appropriate curse words.

The next pitch came screaming in. Again, I swung at nothing. But an earsplitting ping popped off my aluminum bat. Now deaf, startled, and clueless, the instinct to stay alive took over, and I scampered toward first base as if a salivating dog from hell was biting at my legs and ass.

I didn't glance up until I rounded first base, right in time to see their center fielder fumbling to secure the ball after it bounced off the middle of the fence on the fly and took a hard bounce left. By the time he chased the ball down, the three runners on base had crossed the plate. Game over. We won. 3–2.

The players and coaches erupted, screaming, jumping up and down like they'd lost their minds. Then they stopped, spotted me, and charged. They hoisted me up like a sack of turf seed and paraded me around the field. All the horrible, faithless family members in attendance stormed the field too and joined in on the pandemonium.

I got sucked into a daze and started shaking, fighting off the urge to sob with joy. But once the raw exhilaration of the moment burst through the thick walls constructed around my nerve center, a flood of warm, blissful streaks began streaming down my face, but not before they flooded over and through those walls, washing away all the coiled misgivings skulking in the conscious filth behind them.

I continued to gush and blubber and didn't want to stop. Because, as silly and weak as I presented myself after experiencing an uplifting moment, this was my brain's first exposure to the sensation of having every cell inside it charged up with the same kind of super juice the world's most extraordinary people harness to make history.

Because my dad lived in California, he didn't make the trip to Texas for the tournament or the hundred games before it. So, I didn't call him for over a week after our team got knocked out by a talented and scrappy squad we respected but lost to in a hard-fought game, ending our season.

Delaying the call had less to do with juvenile spite than cultured futility. Trying to recreate the towering high of my sporting moment, I reasoned, would be a lumbering nonstarter. So, why bother? To bask in the warmth of his disinterest? Not a chance. If I wanted an animated reaction, loving or otherwise, I'd go sing show tunes at a biker bar.

When he answered my call, I minded the abrasive tone expressing his dark mood. He spoke heavy and slow. After all, it was a Saturday afternoon in sunny Santa Barbara. The ideal time and place for him to skim the back jacket of a new book about Vietnam or meditate on his favorite passages from *The Shining*. A book with more dog-eared pages than Ted Kaczynski's copy of *The Joy of Bombing*.

Crumbling under the weight of muted silence, despite knowing better, I tried regaling him with the theatrical details relating to my swashbuckling summer story of youthful redemption. When I deserted my team like a turncoat to party with Van Halen and got blacklisted by the coach like a Hollywood writer dabbling in communist ideals.

I told him how I stayed positive, remained a supportive team-mate, and managed to deliver the goods when they called my number in the darkest hour. The vacant whir on the line signaled his utter discontent. He drew out a long-suffering sigh and remained silent, only now was impossibly quieter.

I didn't expect him to leap through the phone line and serve up a nourishing platter of homespun kudos with a side of practical know-how, like the tricks he picked up along the path to becoming a man, starting back when he, too, was a well-meaning but clueless kid like me. But I guess the chef's daily special was a seared flank of silent contempt paired with a lovely little side of steamed reproach. Bon appétit, you heavy metal bastard.

What happened to my dad's legendary sense of humor? I thought a joke about the bearded pitcher might suss it out and revive this miscarried exchange, turning the ominous call into an honest-to-goodness Hallmark moment shared between a father and son.

But I also reckoned somewhere out there in this vast, topsy-turvy world lived a long-suffering priest who still cringes to the point of renouncing his faith, thinking about the time he read the last rights to a serial killer on death row as Donald Duck—his earnest but unsuccessful attempt to lift the inmate's bummed-out mood as the disbelieving guards strapped him to the chair.

What could my observational yuks about the bearded twelve-year-old mutant do besides stretch the anxiety of the moment to its ripping point?

After hanging up, I sat in my room for a while—angry, sad, and confused. I put Van Halen's cassette tape *Fair Warning* into my stereo and pressed play. In my head, I cycled through the events of the summer over and over. If given another chance, would I make the same decision? Would anybody care?

Midway through the song "Unchained," I got myself to shut up long enough to get lost in the music. Eddie and the boys were telling me I couldn't get there from here, baby. It was time to stop asking for permission since it was my chance to fly.

Interesting. I wondered if this sound advice helped guide the bearded pitcher's life. Conceivably ballsy statements like these inspired him to stop shaving and gobble up steroids like an ant-eater and were the reason every single mom in the stands cheering him was pregnant with his prison-bound son.

This all sounded sensible in the emancipating context of self-indulgent rock and roll, and might stand out from the other gibberish I scribbled down on paper, but I understood how my cagey mind worked. The bulk of my brain's computing power cycled through programs calculating the ascending gradient of my esteem's slope, solving for the imbalanced ratios projected in my dread's quantum yield, and running defensive simulations to prepare myself for preteen acne's looming attack.

As a result, I couldn't consider Van Halen's sage advice any more than if it suggested I move to Mars, split a twelve-pack with Big Foot, or ask Bo Derek to the school dance.

On the other hand, the directive lyrics in their latest, unremarkable song "Jump" were easier to understand and act on than a midnight infomercial hawking the Clapper.

Go ahead and jump, jump!

HACK TO SCHOOL

Besides playing baseball and hanging out at the beach, going to the movies topped my list of favorite things to do when I still thought of myself as a kid. I went to everything Hollywood rolled out. And I always conveyed my respect and admiration for the film, including hot garbage like *Roller Boogie* and *Logan's Run*, by paying close attention to the story unfolding on-screen and shutting my mouth.

In the '70s, when Hollywood started making tentpole block-busters like *Star Wars* and *Superman*, my family, while still intact, immersed ourselves into the entire moviegoing experience. This was a meaningful way to spend time in Southern California, the only place outside of New York where a studio movie's premiere evoked an elevated level of reverence in the audience, eliciting sensations more associated with joining a cult.

My family believed movies like this deserved to be seen on the city's most enormous screen. We deemed watching the best efforts of Hollywood play out on compact screens at a Cineplex jammed inside a mall as a disgrace. The boorish culinary equivalent of pouring ketchup on a T-bone steak.

The first time Darth Vader appeared on the screen, I covered my eyes. But I couldn't muffle out the sinister sounds of Lord Vader's troubled breathing or the wicked timbre of his commanding voice. But before I ran screaming out of the theater, R2-D2's playful blips and beeps gave me the courage to peek back up at the screen. I'm glad I did. Because what I experienced over the next two hours took movies from something I enjoyed and turned them into a breathing and thinking part of my conscious life. Somehow, *Star Wars* got better after seeing the masterpiece thirteen times.

At this point, most of my regular nightmares drew inspiration from the terrifying things on television, like terrorist attacks, baby seals getting clubbed, and Telly Savalas prancing around wearing nylon shorts on *Battle of the Network Stars*. But the day *Alien* arrived in theaters, every hideous moving image fabricated on screens before it regressed into scenes more calming than soft-focused clips of Bob Ross crosshatching a cluster of emerald pine trees in comparison.

When the heinous baby alien burst out of John Hurt's chest like his bones shared the durability of materials used to build pop-up clown boxes in Tijuana, I shrieked like my ear got pinched by pliers. I yelped through nightmares lasting a year, which only stopped after laughing myself dizzy in a theater watching *Airplane*.

After we moved to Texas, I learned people went to the movies as more of an afterthought, like when no football was on the tube or the weather got too hot to smoke a brisket and shoot stuff.

Soon, the happiness I found inside movie theaters dissolved into a shadowy relic from my unfashionable childhood. At least the misfits I fell in with cared about my well-being. They offered to rewire my brain's pleasure center free of charge, starting with a chemical stripping of my natural perspective, a botched attempt to burn away the residual affection and wonder I had for movies and the magical people who made them.

Despite clinging to my cinematic ideals, I grew to hate Fridays, the usual night we went to the movies. I always went along with a fool's hope things might change. Plus, I was a teenager. Meaning unless my long-term goal revolved around becoming the next Norman Bates, staying home on a Friday night was a nonstarter.

The new and improved movie night routine played out with all the stereotyped inventiveness of a ticking bomb in the trunk of a clueless hero's car. Our night started when we got dropped off in front of the theater by one of our oblivious parents. The second their taillights disappeared, we hustled over to a corner store.

Next, we canvassed the corruptible dregs coming and going until we spotted the perfect kind of iffy creep who was more than happy to buy a roaming troop of underage kids a lawless trove of cheap beer and two packs of Marlboro Lights. Once we made the exchange of cash for beer, we hauled our score behind the theater, huddled around a dumpster, and sucked every can dry like a troupe of B-movie vampires dependent on hops and barley to survive.

After getting buzzed, we bought tickets to the show and shuffled into whatever theater had the most open seats. Topping the long list of the things I hated about this was we were always late to the movie and missed the previews. Plus, since I gave most of my allowance to a pervert in exchange for second-rate beer, I never had enough cash left over to blow on Milk Duds, a tub of buttered popcorn, and an overpriced Coke.

In my old world, these three items were essential components of an authentic moviegoing experience. No less critical than a theater's darkness, cool air, and the collective silence of a respectful audience.

On the other hand, with their heads flooded with cut-rate beer, my friends treated the sacred space inside a theater as their personal lounge. Their incessant yapping only stopped when they busted out laughing at something off-screen or when they stood up and announced, to the delight of the theater's patrons, each time they had to flood the toilet with beer piss.

I longed for my unfashionable childhood, when slipping into the stories on the screen and disappearing from life required all the effort of plopping down in a theater's chair. Now I exhausted myself, bristling with the anxious grief imposed by my friends' never-ending game of movie-night monkey business.

The act of going to the movies now made me imagine an arrangement of snippets pulled together as a sneak preview to promote an upcoming film about a recalcitrant teen's miserable life. A clumsy and predictable knockoff about a boy named Jason Mason trying to find his way in the aftermath of divorce. *Pretty in Drink? Whiskey Business? Canned by Me?* Based on the dailies seen thus far, it's a good bet I'd be watching the Oscars wearing pajamas.

The movie *Back to School* came out in 1986. I loved *Caddyshack*, and Rodney Dangerfield's epic performance earned him a shot to carry a film as its headlining star. *Back to School* opened to solid if not gushing reviews. Many critics compared the movie with the best comedies ever made, pointing out the broad comedy's real beating heart. I counted the days down to the movie's premiere.

On the other hand, my buddies couldn't wait to drink, sit in a dark room, and make everyone around them wish they were either home watching *Full House* or in possession of a loaded gun. But for this movie, I made plans to break off from the pack once we got dropped off, confident nobody would make out my absence or give one squeaky frog's fart if they did.

But this night, one of my friends swiped a nickel bag of weed from the glove box in his older brother's car. And since their simple plan was to smoke the grass right away, my simple plan collapsed because I was too much of a pussy to say no. All the minutes I factored into making this night perfect melted away on shuffling around behind buildings and cars in the parking lot looking for an ideal spot to smoke the weed, something none of us had ever done.

After utilizing the maximum collective capacity of our affiliated brains, we ended up back by the usual dumpster where we always drank beer. Brilliant. The boy with the grass twisted a crude joint, which ended up looking more like convenience store trash picked off the floor of a city bus. But nobody else cared, so we blazed up and passed it around.

I took a puff—okay, three—triggering me to utilize a common reflex, in this case coughing, to separate my rib bones from their corresponding muscle fibers. After the struggle, the mythical stroke of weed's buzz didn't visit. So, besides outrage caused from wasting precious screen time, I felt nothing at all.

When we entered the theater, the movie, of course, had already started. Missing previews is one thing. But missing the start of a film? You might as well start a book on the last page and find out exactly when and how you'll die.

Granted, *Back to School* had little in common with *Murder on the Orient Express*. So, I picked up on the wealthy fish-out-of-water concept quick enough to make sense of the plot. But I couldn't shake the frustrations tied to the lousy seat I sat in, stuffed against the aisle and on the front row, and how the people I considered friends collectively couldn't have cared less.

When the movie ended, as usual, we didn't discuss it. I had thoughts to share and plenty of questions around the plausibility of Thornton Melon's Triple Lindy circus dive. Not to mention the laughable idea Jason Melon, Thornton's son, the whiny little rat-faced twerp who hates being stinking rich, could score a date with the stunning, corn-fed beauty queen, Valerie Desmond. But the recap conversation always revolved around ways to find more beer.

A week later, I went for a second viewing. I was by myself and happy to be alone with a buttery tub of hot popcorn sitting in my lap. Seeing *Back to School* this way reaffirmed my faith in the art of consuming movies.

I noted how the filmmaker used old black-and-white photos to create a brilliant opening montage to lay out the narrative foundation beneath Thornton Melon's rags-to-riches story. Included in the montage were a couple of pictures of a young man posing on the pier in an Atlantic City diving show, planting the seed for Thornton's ability to execute the fabled Triple Lindy, which bloomed and paid off in the movie's dramatic climax.

When I left the theater, I walked home and started questioning the glaring plot weaknesses in my own life's story. As a director, what clips could I mash together to tip off an audience to make how I behaved today pay off later in life? If only my parents took pictures of me pulling whiskers on a pit bull or studying the ingredients used in bleach.

Considering parts of my life to revise or cut out altogether made for a contemplative walk. Of course, I didn't have the guts to fire the current cast of crackpots playing my friends and lacked the authority to shut down production until a better shooting location became available.

But if I somehow pulled off both, unless I addressed the most substantial problem in my story, which was how my chest compared to William Zabka's, the uninspired narrative of my life, I figured, would continue making less sense than *Howard the Duck*.

WASHED
OUT

The summer before my freshman year of high school, when my friends and I weren't deconstructing the Freudian elements threaded through Friday night's movie, we bounded around city fields sweating buckets and playing summer league ball.

Earlier in the spring, my love of the game went missing. All the sweltering, miserable Texas heat did was cause me to call off the search. I held on to a shifty gumshoe's hunch, estimating my love of the game had scurried off to Waco and was slumming around, or buried under, a druggie flophouse near the Little League fields, the last place anyone recalls spotting it.

Over the past couple of years, I had made various attempts to broker my runaway love's comeback, but nothing materialized. All I came across were unsettling reminders magnifying a dreamy past, which stained my heart black. Making me spiteful and ashamed, I fell for baseball's predatory advances as a starry-eyed pleaser, easier to rip open than a bag of ballpark peanuts.

Enough time had passed for me to consider the equation solving for finding lost love is flawed math. Because to be found requires physical actuality and material existence. An object must hold definable characteristics, more than a soppy ideal conjured up by romantic dimwits to delay the escalating horrors gobbling up what's left of their unfeeling lives.

Later in college, I learned the sensation of love was a routine psychological occurrence, like a survival mechanism embedded in the human psyche. A reflex triggered by either hitting rock bottom or having an aneurysm while getting a hand job in Niagara Falls. This reaction allows for the temporary expansion of our limited mental capacity and makes the hypothetical concept of love, or other rosy imaginings like the accuracy of vanity-sized pants, as tangible to humans as a scorpion's sting. I believe the clinical term is cognitive dissonance.

In the end, whether or not my love for baseball was real or generated by the upbeat part of my brain, which prodded me to scan city maps for *Sesame Street*, failed to matter. I was too drained to care.

One night before another dreaded summer game, a friend's

parents left town, and his older brother decided to throw a party. I prayed for him to order three kegs and hire a band, but the gathering turned out to be intimate, with only the coolest of the cool getting invites.

Best of all, they bought enough beer and liquor to satiate Keith Whitley in the off chance his tour bus crashed through their living room. I appreciated being included, unconcerned my participation was contingent on being an expendable pal with his little brother.

I idolized these older guys. So in their honor, I started drinking fast, rifling down four beers before anyone finished their first, which I guess they respected. I moved on from the beer and grabbed a bottle of Jack Daniel's, which I had never drank before. I took a slug from the bottle and gagged. One of the guys told me to mix the whiskey with Coke. I decided better and instead stirred in cherry Kool-Aid with a handful of ice.

I lost track of time, but at some point, the intimate gathering turned into a full-blown bash, and I was screaming through space like a super rocket. This new and improved version of me was fantastic—a fearless badass oozing with charm. And more handsome than I ever dreamed of being since my boyish appeal had a knack of getting smothered under the dark weight of my waking life's ugly disposition.

Now, more puffed up than Sinatra strutting back onstage for an encore, the better me zeroed in on the older girls and slid over to where they were, like the floor was a skating rink created with frozen gin.

These were the same beautiful yearbook goddesses with permed hair and heavy lipstick the factory-made version of me had trouble making eye contact with whenever I bumped into them strutting through the mall shopping for neon hair bows and bleached denim miniskirts.

Now I was chatting them up and making them laugh with the easygoing manner of a playboy who had somehow gotten laid before birth.

I was positive these soon-to-be senior stunners, all giddy and giggling, found me irresistible and impossible not to screw. They had no choice. I was as dashing as a Spanish prince and armed with an excitable quick wit, new to them unless they all met Robin Williams during a three-night coke party hosted at a secluded bungalow tucked up in the Hollywood Hills.

But in less time needed for a sedated Nancy Reagan to mumble, "Just say no," the jeweled crown on my head slipped off and landed near the spot where my ability to speak already crashed. In terms of intelligible lucidity, my voice sat wedged between Marlee Matlin and Chewbacca performing in a cruise line production of A.R. Gurney's Pulitzer Prize–winning play *Love Letters*.

I decided to go swimming and staggered out to the backyard and did a cannonball into the pool. Once I sank to the bottom of the pool, I sat frozen, like a corpse dumped in a lake. I realized I was well past drunk, if not billions and billions of light-years past the last planet I crashed into.

Compared to this, the California Cooler incident was a

whimsical blip of juvenile high jinks, an innocent coming-of-age mishap, plot fodder for an educational episode of an otherwise tone-deaf sitcom built with reprocessed jokes and gags used to mock the unchecked defeatism rotting the lumpy hearts of America's middle class.

I guess I learned my lesson about drinking, Dad.

Super! So, how about you and I have a real drink now, son?

Dad, are you crazy?

Son, I'm talking about ginger ale!

Aww, Dad...

Cue the laugh track and hokey theme song. Fade to black.

My clothes, soaked with water, weighed ten tons. I couldn't move my arms or legs. My panic turned into a maddening realization I was either physically incapacitated, or I had traded bodies with one of the McGuire twins.

By the time my eyes focused, the underwater world turned pleasant and dreamy. I casually observed my deepest, most searing concerns waddle out of the pool in a clumsy rush like they feared what was coming.

I started to think about the only best friend I ever had, my real friend, Doug, who I assumed still lived back in Southern California. We had a carefree friendship built around being comfortable and close. I pictured his house. His family lived in a massive hilltop home with a pool and a tennis court in their expansive backyard. Whenever I stayed the night, we spent all day swimming and playing tennis until wiping out. Afterward, we stayed up late watching movies, trading *Star Wars* cards, and discussing everything from college football (he was an avid USC fan) to the cute girls in our third-grade class, a new and riveting topic.

Doug was the youngest member of a close-knit family of four. They were a jovial clan, affectionate and radiating with a warm light soothing to a kid in my predicament. Meals got prepared and were eaten together, and they played an enviable number of board games as a family, including on weeknights. I marveled at the ease with which they wove into each other's conversations, like a well-tuned jazz band.

Throughout our friendship, acknowledging the glaring differences between our families exposed clues indicating perhaps mine was flawed. If Doug's family was a jazz quartet doing a tight set at Preservation Hall, mine was more like an inexperienced western band playing their first gig at a rowdy swamp bar, unable to finish one full song due to the broken glass exploding through the chicken wire wrapped around the stage as a makeshift but ineffective barrier erected to keep performers like us from getting killed.

I had plenty of friends in Texas, but anytime I thought about the enjoyable and innocent times I used to have with Doug, I came close to tears. I missed having a best friend.

"Pull him out! Pull him out! Is he breathing?" somebody yelled.

I came back to life. After a slow peek around, I recognized my friend's backyard, but I was puzzled about being laid out in the grass next to the pool, soaked and limp as a dishrag. And why was I surrounded by party guests wearing the same shocked expression people put on when their pet poodle is bleeding out in the middle of a busy street?

I remembered grabbing the bottle of Jack Daniel's. Beyond that brilliant moment, my brain's security footage played blank. Not ideal. But the clear image of me standing on the mound in less than five hours was much worse.

Hours later, heading to the game, I dug deep to keep from throwing up all over the back of my mom's car. The last few years had ravaged what remained of my faith, which, including the halcyon days of my shiny California youth, was shaky at best. So, I didn't have an opinion on if what happened next was pure dumb luck or the work of God's hand. But the clouds turned dark, the wind picked up, and rain started falling in buckets.

If I had paid attention in Sunday school, I might've made the connection to the spiteful frogs falling from the sky in Exodus 8. But I doubt it, because today, after watching the movie *Magnolia* no less than ten times with a sharp, determined focus, I have no clue if a flood of slimy bullfrogs falling from the sky is an agreeable omen or a sloppy hint from the man above indicating the end is nigh.

As we sat in the car waiting for the ref to cancel the game, I stared at the rain, dismayed and speechless, like an overheated desert nomad looking at a glass filled with cold water. But inside this dumbfounded state, I recognized I needed to shift course and make substantial changes in my life. Right now.

Soon, officials canceled the game. I never appreciated the size of the bullet I dodged because I avoided looking back long enough to find out. But the event revealed a fork in destiny's road. Knowing my life was at risk forced me to decide fast on which route to take.

SPRING LOADED

I found myself accelerating down this new path, unconcerned with the expanding distance between me and everything I grew up glorifying, like baseball, brainy grades, and making sure my ridiculous plaid shirts got starched so stiff they might shatter on a carpeted floor if dropped. All this before eating lunch during my first day of high school.

On this enlightened path, the thought of hauling trash for a living when I graduated didn't bother me. Besides, those guys got plenty of sunshine and cleared $25K per year. Assuming the absence of an invincible addiction to back-alley crystal meth, these liberated men make plenty of cash to live an everyday life, which, at this point, was all I wanted.

Nevertheless, an ascending vision of the future turned up on the side of the road whenever I veered too far off course. Helping me also came via the decade of record. The '80s. The greed decade. The instance of measured time blessing the world with an infinite supply of visual examples to help identify characteristics embedded in lost causes. Think glam metal, stone-washed jeans, and the movie *Ishtar*. And whatever part of me delegated the final say concerning my place in the world refused to acknowledge the conspicuous markings of a doomed loser as seen anytime I glanced in a mirror.

After the first semester of high school, I spent my entire Christmas break getting admonished for bringing home a report card distinguished by below-average grades. I listened long enough and found motivation in the idea of leveraging stellar grades to thwart my mom's spirited attacks, demolishing my overall character.

This triggered the drawing up of a strategic counter initiative to weaponize my classroom grades, potentially giving me the leverage needed to regain control of the house narrative, if not my life.

I presented my plan's details before returning to school. Pitching my idea with the decided confidence of a slick salesman explaining the benefits of a life raft to a group of passengers on the Titanic. In short, if I got straight As during the first reporting period, a spring break trip with my friend's family to South Padre Island counted as my reward. I made her an offer she couldn't refuse.

I'm not criticizing my mom's ability to negotiate. But we were California people. To her, going to the beach meant splashing around in the waves, tossing a Nerf football, and taking long naps on the sand under the delightful Southern California sun. Still new enough to Texas, my mom's knowledge about spring break pastimes along the Texas coast remained exploitable. Blissfully unaware college kids from every state swarmed to Padre, determined to create moments sure to make the wildest times aboard Van Halen's private jet get mistaken for a Tupperware party held in a church next to the nursery during nap time.

But it's possible her understanding of spring break mischief classified as absolute. And she only agreed to the deal believing an orphan holding a steerage ticket on the Titanic had a better chance of seeing New York's skyline than she did of seeing perfect marks printed on my report card. Whatever the case, once we shook hands, I transformed myself into a super nerd.

Of course, I withheld one piece of information from the deal's contract. The detail rated so low in significance, I figured, why bother? If I did win the bet, I wouldn't be going on a spring break beach trip with my friend's family exactly, but rather his older brother, a fun-loving college freshman at a top Texas party school.

To me, an avid fan of LA Law, I concluded the word "family" covered the contract's legal intent well enough, in the event we clashed in family court to obtain a ruling. Also missing from the enforceable document was the fact my friend's older brother might bring along ten of his SAE pledge class buddies, known for making

Robert Downey Jr.'s wildest night look like a craft brew tasting. I reasoned unsubstantial speculation like this deemed excessive for a legitimate and binding legal agreement. And too much studying sat in front of me to consider the matter any further.

I made this academic wager to oppress my academic aggressor, but my motivation's initial spark to earn a spot on the honor roll came from the bright lights of Hollywood. I watched every spring break movie made to honor and sentimentalize this sacred week no less than a thousand times: *Fraternity Vacation*, *Hardbodies*, and the cleverly titled *Spring Break*.

Sure, the copy written on the side of an airplane's barf bag carried more depth than every spring break movie script combined, but I didn't care. I loved them. To me, these films constituted more than ridiculous and raunchy romps. Because behind all the foam and flesh, I discovered, in these movies, the presence of an empowering undercurrent of innocent hope fused to a vexing possibility of acquiring and ingesting the magical elixir you'd been raised to believe existed, but only for those with better breeding. But if you start believing in yourself enough to fight back, your hands, too, shall soon caress the golden chalice brimming with thy mystical tonic. Or in this case, Coors Light.

Whenever a spring break movie played, I viewed the moving pictures on-screen in an imaginative trance, frozen by tender longing. The FBI best describes this mental and physical state in reports detailing John Hinckley's behavior watching Jodie Foster marathons on AMC.

Now, the only thing blocking me from my spring break destiny cumulated in my ability to pull in straight As at a public high school regarded nationally by academic watchdogs to be a total joke.

The drive to South Padre took nine hours. We made the trek in a custom-made van one of the fraternity brothers borrowed from a creepy bozo of an uncle—or so I assumed two seconds after stepping inside.

The van's musty interior flaunted more fake pinewood and plush carpet than a roadside motel. All tied together by a sturdy color scheme, like a poster saluting parts of America where leaves changed colors and a man's handshake meant more than a contract.

But the interior's incidental connection to the Midwest's prudent design sensibilities came undone when the nonbookworm college boy sitting next to me cracked open a cold beer and washed down two hits of ecstasy. *Interesting breakfast choice,* I thought. But not shocking. In the late '80s, glamour drugs like cocaine and X carried the same risk as breath mints and were deemed harmless by a board of medical professionals practicing in Florida, safer to humans than aspirin powder mixed into butterscotch pudding.

He offered me a hit with a jarring sense of nonchalance, like handing out a stick of gum. Appreciative, but I declined as I grabbed my first beer. The clock on the radio displayed the time—9:14 a.m.

Over the next eight hours, I drank enough beer to lose count. Without consequence, the freedom to drink without hiding behind a movie theater dumpster like a common thief proved exhilarating.

Moreover, drinking this many beers nonstop might've also saved my life. Otherwise, I might've hung myself like the nun in the movie *Airplane*. Because for the entirety of the trip, the traveling companion next to me spoke at the same pace and volume as a livestock auctioneer fortified with a bucket of truck stop coffee and never paused long enough to take a breath.

I detected no reason to complain, for these young princes consented to transport me into a new world, giving the generative experience of starring in my own '80s-style spring break movie the green light. I owed it to them and my fellow peers to produce a memorable hit.

```
     SPRING LOADED
     (A TREATMENT)


     by Jason Carter


Logline: An increasingly confused and contem-
plative high school freshman seeks the meaning
of life during the wildest week of the year,
spring break!
   Synopsis: JASON is a decent kid coming
to grips with his less-than-ideal child-
hood. Divorce. Getting dragged away from his
```

beloved home in California. Changing schools
more often than an Army brat. And now he
realizes nothing matters anyhow, and life
is a long and erratic slog.

But dealing with all the touchy and intro-
spective hogwash eventually exhausted him,
inspiring a journey to find the meaning of
life. And the best and only place such purpose might be found, he reasoned, was along
the Texas coastline during the second week of
March, when the lusty shenanigans associated
with spring break were in full swing.

After an eye-opening nine-hour ride in a
custom van with zany frat guys, he arrives at
the magical beach house. He and his friend
race to a keg, drink beer until they puke,
and soon pass out under the scorching sun.

The next day, looking like lobsters, they
hook up with kids their own age. One of these
kids had been sent off to a military school
created for rich delinquents. And he soon
proves why by pulling out a massive joint
the size of a hammer's handle, and they all
start smoking.

Now, bombed, they crash a college party, race to a keg, drink beer until they puke, and pass out under the glittering stars.

The next day, Jason tries his luck with a ridiculously bogus fake ID he bought back home at a makeshift flea market. He tries to enter a raging bar filled with beautiful college girls but gets laughed at by the bouncer and, worse, laughed at by a group of beautiful college girls.

Humiliated, he and his friends decide to hitch a ride to the border town of Matamoros, Mexico, which is only thirty minutes away. Of course, the person who drives them to Mexico is a zany mentor with sage advice. (Think Bob Newhart in a hilarious cameo!)

Remember, kids. Worms are for fishing hooks.

Now among the thousands and thousands of drunk college kids flooding the streets and cantinas, they head into a bar, only this time, they drink tequila until they puke and soon pass out on a gross bathroom floor.

The next day, looking a little haggard, Jason meets a beautiful college girl at a keg party on the beach. He lies to her.

My name is Preston. I go to Duke.

Soon, he has her giggling like a girl petting a barking seal at the zoo. They're having fun. She's buying into his synthetic charm.

He goes to refill their beers from a keg, where he tells his wasted friends he's in love. His friends are impressed he wooed a beautiful college girl.

Great, did you see her tits?

Jason, so mature and wise, walks off.

Grow up, children.

Jason, now floating, goes back to the girl with two full beers. But he freezes, his face contorts to suggest a sharp pain in his heart, and in slow motion, he drops the beers.

Because now his future wife is aggressively making out with and grinding all over a massive college football player.

She makes unapologetic eye contact with Jason, and hell gets hotter when she grabs two handfuls of this meaty college football

player's fat ass and gives his steaming hot
beach buns a hard and filthy squeeze.

Crushed, heartbroken, and devastated,
Jason goes back to his friends. They go to
a keg, drink beer until they puke, and soon
pass out near the swimming pool.

On the last night of spring break, the
older guys are prepping the beach house for
an epic party. They have kegs, trash can
punch, and a tall bong.

Jason looks like the personification of
hell. He takes a sip of beer and gags.

As he considers healthier life choices
(via an internal montage backed by Falco's
"Rock Me Amadeus" that shows him jogging,
working out, eating a salad, and reading *The
Righteous Purity of Life!* by Jimmy Swaggart.

The drugged-up frat guy he sat next to
in the custom van on the way down comes over
and hands him a pill.

Jason examines the pill and then washes
the drug down with beer.

Jason is happy, dancing like he recently
passed a kidney stone the size of a bowling

ball and bear-hugging anyone unlucky enough
to be standing nearby.

Notable are the appearance of his pupils,
which share the size, shape, and coloring
of a charcoal briquette.

The beautiful college girl who broke his
heart comes into the party, hanging all
over the dopey college football player.
Jason stops cold. He signals his friends
and nods.

He grabs a full plastic cup of beer and
approaches his dream girl, who is running
her whorish hands all over this sex-crazed
buffoon.

"Remember me, Preston from Duke?"

Her blank and annoyed expression says it
all. "Uh, yeah. But, like, I'm trying to
forget."

"Oh, really?" Jason smashes the full beer
into the idiot college football player's face.
"Good luck with that." And runs for his life.

Sunrise.

Jason wakes up outside, somewhere between
two dunes. His shirt is gone, and he's

shivering. He gets up and stumbles toward the
beach house.

The expression on his face can best be
described as whatever signifies an emotion a
million times sadder than the face of a boy
getting the news his pet dog lost all four
of his furry little legs under grandpappy's
riding mower.

The next scene shows the custom van pulling out of the driveway in front of the beach
house—time to head home.

In the van, Jason sits by the same guy he
sat next to on the way down, who looks like
a pickled corpse, frowning.

Back outside. The van crosses the bridge
back to the mainland for what's sure to be a
long and miserable ride home.

Back in the van, everyone is passed out
except for Jason. He's staring out the window at nothing, with a haunting blankness on
his face projecting the thought, *I'm done
searching*.

And the peppy hit "Manic Monday" by the
Bangles starts playing as the camera pulls

in closer and closer to Jason's lifeless
face until we're blinded by the blackness
of his right pupil.

                              FADE TO BLACK.

13

YOUNG LIVES

Young Life is a Christian ministry established in 1941 to lure wayward teens into God's fold by reducing the formidable stories told in the Bible down into sunny, childlike songs composed using the same three chords any circus monkey can pluck on his banjo.

The tax-exempt organization hosted spirited rallies in school gymnasiums or whatever nondescript, commercial-sized hall offered their useable space at no cost. And any nonfelon, scruffy Christian-type in their twenties in possession of a concert T-shirt promoting Journey or Abba, faded jeans, and a secondhand guitar might find themselves getting fast-tracked into a leadership role.

If God sent me a profound message during these rallies, his sound advice got lost in the skeptical muck slinking through my mind. But a curious number of teenagers treated these rallies with genuine, God-fearing reverence. They arrived early, rushing to secure prime seats, as if their lives depended on sitting in the front row. And once the show began, they sang like baby birds squeaking at worms hanging from their mother's beak.

Watching them sing, hold hands, and rock back and forth, smiling ear to ear, I grappled with the impossible idea these white-washed kids were grateful for the quality of their lives. And on the rare occasion any one of them thought beyond the protective imaginings of sweet peaches soaking in cream, they came here, joined hands, and sang those pesky blues away.

But I didn't buy it. Instead, I chose to believe anyone my age prancing around with a toothy smile, eager to sing hokey songs while holding hands, indicated something sinister lurked in the shadowy background of their willy-nilly lives. Then again, it's possible they got baked to Baltimore (for all I knew) and bonked their ears off in the broom closet before every show. The only thing I knew for sure is whatever they took to trip on arrived uncut, not stepped on a hundred times like the gritty dust in my bag.

My friends and I took part in these rallies to avoid being home and to check for cute girls in the crowd from other schools. But the spiritual payoff for participating turned up when our tickets got punched for Young Life's annual spring break ski trip.

Considering my spring break trip to the beach the previous

year, the idea of screaming down the slopes with Jesus made for a prudent choice. Besides, what's the worst existing consequence designed to punish troublemakers making merry on a Bible-based boondoggle to the mountains? Eternal banishment from the ice cream bar? Sign me up.

The trip's destination was a no-frills ski resort outside of Durango, Colorado, called Purgatory. I figured the metaphorical obsession propelling Young Life's leadership decision-making process goaded them to choose Purgatory to help prop up the trip's flimsy theme. And gosh, I wondered, is "purgatory" more than an average mountain for irredeemable teens to swoop down stoned on skis? Would we sing songs explaining how "purgatory" also functioned as an intermediate holding tank where wayward souls are jailed after croaking? And learn how in Purgatory, wretched souls stand nude in front of a power hose until their bare asses shine brighter than a polished halo, making Peter glad to wave them through heaven's gate. Wow. And all I expected out of Purgatory was average snow.

When the buses pulled into the hotel's parking lot after a twenty-hour drive, most of the kids darted to the ski shop for boot fittings or raced to take a shower before the hotel's water heater conked out (which they warned us about). My friends and I strolled off the bus and up to our room to start setting up the bar.

A few of us crossed the street to a liquor store. Each experienced in grinding the organ like a street monkey for strangers and creeps, dazzling them into tossing coins into Master Alcohol's cap. So, it didn't take long to impress a passerby of legal age, who agreed to pay us in favor by using our parents' money to purchase an obscene amount of alcohol for stocking the bar.

Of course, the holy rollers in charge communicated to us, our parents, and the ex-con driving the bus: if anyone drank alcohol, they got shipped straight home riding the bus of shame, and afterward, they would burn eternal in hell. No questions asked. As usual, we treated this stern warning with the same deference of being told to never chew gum in class.

Once the bar opened for business, we unfastened the room's windows, lit cigarettes, and started mixing drinks strong enough to power a two-stroke engine. At the time, I didn't deliberate the thoughts racing through God's head as he checked in on us, but I bet he did a holy-water spit-take. *Are you kidding me with these clowns? I named the damn mountain Purgatory!*

An alarming series of loud *thump, thump, thumps* made us jump. *What the hell?* The pounding continued. One of my friends peered through the peephole and quickly turned whiter than the snow outside blanketing the ground.

The unwelcome visitor turned out to be one of Young Life's foot soldiers and was well known to be the worst volunteer to stumble into if you happen to be holding a lit cigarette next to more booze than the Rat Pack kept flowing backstage at the Sands.

He distinguished himself as a hard charger by giving us the stink eye one minute after boarding the bus, and his underhanded involvement with Young Life reeked of a long-abandoned come-back. At any rate, he signed on to "mentor" kids the second his greedy dreams of playing squash with Gordon Gekko demateri-alized and vanished faster than his clients' money when the '87 stock market crashed through the floor.

Now he owned nothing and shuttled around less to lose. An acute combination of irreversible misfortune, scientifically proven to turn desperate men into junkies, serial killers, or independent business operators schilling toothpaste and toilet paper for Amway.

As he pounded on the door with an escalating sense of purpose-driven vengeance, nobody moved or exhaled a breath. We must've resembled young soldiers in a spine-chilling photo captured by an unseen war photographer at the exact moment one of them triggered the telling click of a landmine with the heel of his boot. In this case, the subsequent blast (the door opening) would be the end of us.

I couldn't help but scrutinize alcohol's role in this doomed firefight. Obviously, without alcohol, there'd be no war. In a dry world, we might be happy-go-lucky kids unpacking our clothes, waxing up our skis, and checking up on the current movies cycling on HBO. So, was it time for me to reconsider alcohol's increasing prominence in my life?

But before reaching a levelheaded conclusion about booze, the jarring sound of metal hitting the ground destroyed the track freighting my purposeful thoughts. I spun around. One of my friends was busy shoving all the liquor through a massive hole in the wall, which the sheet-metal air vent sitting on the floor covered in ordinary situations.

And as we stood frozen, bug-eyed, each imagining the grisly outcome awaiting our luckless lives, he found and deployed a box fan and started blowing the smoky clouds of synthetic proof out of the room through the open windows.

Next, this friend, Russ, demonstrating the brisk grace of a Russian spy, screwed the vent back into the wall with his pocketknife, then dashed to his shaving bag and whipped out a black bottle of Drakkar Noir. And with the brash flair of a gigolo prepping his workspace for a clammy tussle with a widowed heiress, he squeezed out three quick loads of the provocative mist before returning the world's most depraved cologne to the bag before the first wad of sexy smelling molecules stained the covers.

Hopeful but burning with the cognizant blush of inadequacy, I walked to the door, undid the lock, and let the eager snake slither into our room.

After his five-minute scramble to find alcohol, the non-Gekko, enraged, quit looking. He stood near the door, struck stiff, speechless, and shaking. I imagined this humiliating moment brought him back to the day Wall Street pistol-whipped him and ten thousand other weak-kneed traders across the face. After he slinked out, we erupted.

During our delirious celebration, someone coined the perfect nickname for our heroic friend who saved the day: MacGyver.

A more fitting moniker bestowed on a man exists only in the enchanted imaginations of history's most originating prophets.

MacGyver flawlessly captured his genius-level intellect, proficient engineering skills under pressure, and in an eloquent coincidence, the wavy air-blown locks of sandy brown hair sitting on top of his cunning and beautiful face. Unlike the fate of silly nicknames conjured up and assigned to boys in high school, this denomination established and celebrated the most distinctive attributes supporting his physical and spiritual essence.

More remarkable to me, this moniker did so in a way that surpassed the maximum efficiency of a word's functional capacity, including every bold literary experiment spearheaded by Michael Chabon. The same can't be said about nicknames like Odor Gut, Milk Stain, and Pencil McMicro Dick.

Unfortunately, as perfect as the nickname was, it failed to save his life. Because twenty-eight years later, Russ Reed, a.k.a. MacGyver, one of my dearest friends, drank too much and drowned in shallow water after tripping off a boat dock.

He was forty-two years old and left two sons behind. Twins. Each of them came carved from the same extraordinary mold as their father. These two boys serve as inconceivable proof the heavenly place Russ Reed came from does, in fact, exist.

After Russ's funeral, the people closest to him went to lunch. I sat at the table, sad and too hungover from the night before to speak. The waitress delivered frosty goblets filled with beer to our table fast, and the time between each round shrank from ten minutes to *keep 'em coming* quicker than a face-plant caused by one of the billion patches of ice dotting Purgatory Mountain.

I bristled at the pitch-black irony of trying to outdrink my hangover on today of all days and wondered how many of life's lessons went ignored or forgotten.

Russ always pulled me out of my fights with downward thinking. He holds the champion's belt for making me laugh, and I never met anyone else with enough of the right stuff needed to dethrone the champ. He established no use for dark thoughts, choosing instead to parade the best and brightest moments from his own colorful life out for internal consideration.

Above all else, he and I shared an equal appreciation for humor woven together with the strings of absurdity and darkness. Russ and I found laughs anywhere, and he was quick to share his findings with anyone whose pained heart needed a healing laugh.

So, Russ Reed, my dear boy, here are the quips I scribbled down when we honored your life. I remember wishing, more than anything, you sat next to me and allowed those approving snorts and cackles echoing off your contagious laugh out to play with us one more time.

TOP THREE COMMENTS OVERHEARD
AT MACGYVER'S FUNERAL

1. If only duct tape and wire yanked from
   a toaster floated.
2. And you thought bad ratings were a killer.
3. They didn't call the show MacDiver for
   a reason.

   Rest in peace, dear friend.

DETROIT
SCHLOCK CITY

I n the early '70s, most logical Americans snickered at Detroit's unchecked obsession with size and power, a reckless pursuit recognized by environmental watchdogs as a Freudian disgrace. But Motor City reigned king and sneered at the notion size didn't matter and continued engineering prodigious features exalting the gamy essence of manhood into every aspect of their cars.

Take the Corvette Stingray, for instance. Detroit's prodigal son. Chevrolet's most virile, unrestrained creation. Renowned for the hulking, hyperreactive piece of equipment hanging close to the ground, over a measured foot below a driver's enormous feet.

Built for throttling all comers, once turned on. The Stingray's steamy design (its penetrating length and sensual curves, the visible sheen on the hood induced by the vibrating engine's coiled pulsation) got fast-tracked by GM's new CEO, Richard Gerstenberg. Insiders claim the rush job leaped off Mr. Gerstenberg's desk, ignited by his fondness for group sex and growing obsession with the enduring bulge posted up in Robert Plant's skintight jeans.

Around the same time, OPEC rose to international prominence by decoding how to halt production of the world's oil faster than Richard Nixon's spooks could tap a phone. Now, panicked Americans clubbed each other with bats and pipes to secure their place in line to buy a lifesaving car made in Japan.

Unlike American automobiles, Japanese vehicles celebrated innovation and dependability, and didn't suck up gas like a baleen whale. So, in the event the West Coast got nuked, an expected happening counted down nightly on the local news, a hysterical family fleeing Fresno for Atlanta only needed a half tank of gas to cross Georgia's state line uncooked.

In Detroit, the Big Three continued shrugging off the apocalypse. The thick strands of blind patriotism rooted in their DNA convinced them the trendy metric MPG stood for Meat, Potatoes, and Gravy.

And over a long, sloppy night of stout cocktails inside the Country Club of Detroit, they doubled down. Pledging under a blood oath to update their no-frills fleet of middle-class offerings and give skittish Americans what they needed most—excessive gobs of Motor City muscle.

Of course, this strategic initiative backfired like a stalled Pinto. And the total weight of the automobile industry's economics shifted to the East. Overnight, millions of factory jobs vanished, and Detroit became a place to send the newly dead deserving of a place worse than hell.

But in my mind, these men should've won a Nobel Prize. Because ten years after one of the most irresponsibly engineered asphalt-devouring gas evaporators rolled off the GM line as a direct result of their boozy meeting, the day I turned sixteen, the keys to a 1978 Pontiac Grand Prix fell in my lap.

From the day the car launched, the Grand Prix took critical heat, widely pegged as a yawner. And for good reason. Inside the Grand Prix's engineering rooms, the car's creation became a total joke, driving them to phone it in, any running piece of junk to fool brain-dead American consumers. Specifically, the sluggish grandpa needing a threadbare vehicle for driving to church, bingo, or medical supply outlets with good deals on bedpans and catheter bags.

But my Grand Prix rolled off the line after Detroit's collective mind went mad. Like the Trans Am Burt Reynolds used to flip off the world in *Smokey and the Bandit*, my car gleamed the colors black and gold. Sure, the tan plastic seats held up to genuine leather the way river rocks compare to the Hope Diamond. But the T-tops slivered through the roof helped me look past all the third-degree burns.

But the most brilliant design feature came through the positioning of the car's gear stick. In Grandpa's flaccid Grand Prix, the shifting handle hung out sideways from the steering wheel. As a result, engaging the transmission required pulling the shaft downward. The symbolic equivalent of losing an erection, so spot-on it's a wonder the sad trombone notes of *womp, womp* didn't blow in the background every time some gimpy old-timer shifted into drive.

Alternatively, my gear stick, fused to the car's outrageous EC301 motor, jutted out from the floorboard, straight up and fully erect, like the shifter represented Detroit's plump middle finger at full extension, giving OPEC and every spineless American pansy driving a Honda the bird.

Of course, in 1988, any teenage boy owning a car without a stereo capable of shattering the stained glass out of a church might as well drive a pink tricycle. To this end, I spared no expense.

First, I bought an Alpine deck hot enough to heat crack rocks from a shifty guy at school. Next, I added a two-hundred-watt Sherwood amp to help push the four custom woofers and two six-by-nine speakers beyond the established legal limits of sound and decency. Of course, an upgrade like this required me to lay out an extraordinary amount of money, which drew my savings account down from dollars to cents.

Up to this point, the scope of my understanding regarding financial matters didn't extend past getting correct change at the arcade. But once I calculated the amount of cash needed to keep my Grand Prix running, thanks to Detroit's mighty EC301 engine sucking through fuel like the engineers used chicken wire to build its gas tank, securing a job replaced my fight against acne as priority number one.

This led me to our city's best steakhouse, a legendary place called Mac's House, where I found work as a busboy. Mac's House provided a center of gravity for Fort Worth's fun-loving power players. A food critic once described Mac's House as the perfect place for wildcatters to burn their new riches pouring in after hitting a lucky gusher.

The alluring Waspy vibe of Mac's House permeated through the self-assurance of its high-hat interior design. Dark walls made of stained oak. Sturdy tables covered with white cloths and polished silver. All set under dimmed lights, making the wax candles burning on top of each table the primary source of light and, for many diners, the quickest way to light an after-dinner cigarette.

Most of the loyal and tenured staff started showing up at Mac's House to start a shift when dinosaurs roamed the earth. The waitresses ranged in age from their late forties to early sixties and demonstrated a fanatical zeal for their job more common in suicide bombers because, in the cutthroat world of steakhouse service jobs, this gig spit out the most cash. By far.

Each night, tables stayed full from open to close with the most charismatic and wealthy people in town, and they were more than happy to leave outrageous tips to honor their impeccable service, like hundred-dollar slot machines rigged in their favor.

These women progressed through shifts, displaying similar attributes associated with field generals during a war. Fearless, precise, and unflinching. As they showed me the ropes throughout my first night, I got a sense they didn't care for things like small talk, surplus movement, and human emotions.

But as I familiarized myself with how they flowed through each grueling night of service (in a way I considered too programmatic to be tolerable by most humans), any favorable attempt to understand their tireless commitment to perfection fell short. Instead, I respectfully observed a level of pride and professionalism poured into a craft I never witnessed before or have seen since. These women loved the customers, and the customers loved them right back. These curated relationships between the most divergent types of people forged sincere bonds aglow with meaning.

I realized these dignified and beautiful women could experience the full range of human emotions. But they also possessed an unlimited capacity to affect the worth of others. For this reason, I considered time in their company as privileged and treated the act of earning their friendship and trust as a noble pursuit.

I'm sure Christopher Columbus performed cartwheels when he discovered America. But for him, or anyone capped by the prophetic limitations of the human mind, predicting what would become of the sand his ship slid into through dumb luck was an impossible waste of imaginative time. At Mac's House, I experienced a discovery connected to a similar type of inconceivable future.

On a Tuesday night, after a busier shift than expected, the waitresses and busboys gathered in the back room to rest our feet and split the tips. And in a show of appreciation for my hard work, the waitresses I worked for handed me an unopened bottle of red wine.

On the same night, I needed to write a short story for my English class, due the next day. An assignment haunting me for weeks, all the way up to nut-cutting time—the sequence of events. You see, the act of not writing, paired with a steely determination to create new reasons never to write, doesn't come from being a lazy student. For me, the act of not writing shared more in common with getting boiled alive.

From a young age, sometime between kindergarten and first grade, I decided to be a writer. And despite the telling pile of second- and third-place ribbons handed to me by unimpressed teachers judging the writing contests I entered and lost, my determination to tell stories never flinched. Yet, each time I sat down to write, I froze, too much of a coward to stir up the authentic voice slumbering in the dark caverns of my true self. Not so much by what it said to me, but by people considering what my voice said to them. Fittingly, I feared literary rejection the way others feared getting attacked by sharks or traveling by bus.

When I got home after my shift, the clock said 11:00 p.m. I took a quick shower and sat down at my desk. For a long time, I stared at the blank page under my nose, twirling my pen. Bored, frustrated, and other euphemisms for scared stiff, I peered at the bottle of red wine standing on my desk for a long time the way art collectors stare at a painting hung on a museum wall.

I learned the wine hailed from Spain. The yellow label maintained the texture of a milled paper map like explorers used centuries ago to help navigate the waters toward fanciful worlds thought to exist only in their romantic minds. The image fabricated on the label bespoke an artist's sketch illustrating an early-world sailing ship frozen in time. Crafted to convey the thrill of her pushing into an ominous ocean swell before pioneering out farther, fleeing the ordinary world, which failed to inspire the hearts and minds of the quixotic crew.

I walked to the kitchen and grabbed a corkscrew from a drawer. The waitresses uncorked hundreds of bottles in front of me, but I hadn't popped one open myself. I mangled the cork when I did, leaving small chunks bobbing on top of the red wine's surface like ship wreckage.

I got back to my room, sat down, poured the wine into a tall glass, and let the watery red velvet sit, mimicking people who romanced their wine at the restaurant. Then I brought the glass to my nose and pulled in a deep whiff so sharp and tangy I recoiled. But the mood hovering in the immediate air changed, like a new gust of warm, florid wind blew in, hauling essential scents of vibrancy and life. I smiled. And as the red vapors continued charging out of the bottle and glass, like bulls running on the streets of Spain, all the groggy truth inside me started stirring. I brought the glass to my lips and took a long, healthy gulp.

I woke up the next day in a hotter version of hell. This seafaring queasiness surpassed the worst pangs ever obtained from the simple wreckage associated with cheap beer and bourbon hangovers. My desk lamp was still on, as were my clothes.

Soon, a flood of memories carrying images of my wine-fueled writing tryst washed away the biting fog. In them, I scribbled like mad, bopping my head to jazz and swirling the red wine around in my glass, pouring more until the bottle emptied.

In my flashback, I acted free and brilliant. If not for the lack of unfiltered cigarettes, absinthe, and streams of witty banter, I may as well have been in a Parisian gin house wedged between Hemingway and Gertrude Stein. For the first time in my life, I think, a memory tripped the wires controlling my agreeable emotions.

I hopped out of bed excited to read my outpouring of last night's brilliant prose. But when I got to my desk, I scratched my head, confused and grimacing. Because if not for a few obscure sentences fashioned around the cryptic gibberish of a man gone mad (and apparently written using his opposite hand), the pages would be blank.

Now, instead of a mind-blowing paper, the only thing accompanying me to school would be a mind-bending hangover. My first dance with red wine's aftershock, coincidentally, reminded me of Homer's *The Odyssey*, at least in the sense of feeling utterly confused, if not nauseous, when I read it, while at the same time fearing the misery of doing so would last forever.

But, lucky for me, I attended a public high school, meaning the academic consequences awaiting me, if any existed, worried me less than getting caught chewing gum in class.

But where did all the literary magic go? Something remarkable happened the night before. I knew it. I felt it. For the first time, however brief, the actual writer cowering inside me emerged for a quick peek outside before moving on. I looked forward to rec-reating the alluring scene to bait him out of hiding so we could hang out again.

Only next time, I'd try typing.

A MIRE
EDUCATION

The welcome packet Dartmouth sends to incoming students comes with a handwritten note from the dean, along with a slew of considerate information to ensure the clumsiest freshman's first step on campus finds solid ground, or so I heard.

I applied to schools without care-package programs spearheaded to keep incoming goofs like me from spiraling down the academic and social conduits constructed to drain those unprepared out into mud bogs of poverty, despair, and retail work.

With little support and less to go on, I mapped out my college adventure leveraging resources like questionable instincts and a quarter to flip, resulting in a plan comparable to directions written by a meth addict describing the steps to solve a Rubik's Cube.

For starters, after high school, I chose to spend the better part of summer living in Santa Barbara with my dad. In the ten years since my parents divorced, he and I never spent more than a handful of consecutive nights under the same roof. So, through the application of conservative reasoning, I projected the temperature of situational awkwardness to run hotter than a situation revolving around an irritable mom tweezing deer ticks out of her teen son's beanbag.

Mom! Ouch!

You think I'm enjoying this, you little pervert!

I hate you! Ouch!

All things being equal, I couldn't stomach another summer in Texas. And I figured if the simmering tension between my dad and me boiled into Tobias Wolff's territory, I could crank out a modern-day rip-off of *This Boy's Life* for a pile of cash, college be damned. So naturally, this streak of logical thinking forklifted the idea of attending college in California to the top of my scatterbrained list.

As for anyone suffering under the oppressive regulations enforced by the bloodless defenders of dysfunctional family law, never underestimate the power of time apart. Because for me, by unexpected chance, this obscure workaround made nurturing the wagon loads of bitter recollections about my dad impossible. Akin to growing crops without soil, rain, and earth-defiling pesticides.

Better still, the simmering anxiety produced while anticipating the itchiness of our unnatural reunion, and the consequent, infuriating proximity linked to living under the same roof didn't travel well over the vast physical distance plunked between our lives. As a result, the unsettling doubts stuffed in my luggage all but disappeared by the time I dropped my bags at my dad's front door.

To ensure my college adventure kicked off with an upstanding start, I enrolled in two of the sweetest cakewalk classes offered at Santa Barbara City College. Once the summer semester began, I arrived at campus without knowing a single person. But I soon found being an invisible nobody to be a delightful way to breeze through the day. Freed from the snarls of social obligations, I shifted the most restless parts of my attention to the task of producing respectable grades.

Each morning, I walked to campus from my dad's house through lifting fog, listening to headphones. In class, I took detailed notes and added, I think, some tangible value to the classroom discussions professors encouraged students to join.

After class, I darted home and powered through my assigned reading or memorized notes for an upcoming quiz or exam. When I shut the books, I pedaled my bike down to the beach to jog a few miles barefoot on the sand before diving into the surf for a refreshing swim.

My daily routine made for an agreeable indoctrination into higher learning. The total opposite of the raging, beer-soaked fraternity scene I fantasized about since the time I recognized my college motives at a young age in a story about, um, my dad. *Go Big Red!*

My dad arrived home from work around six, took a shower, and changed into shorts and a Hawaiian shirt. We met up in the kitchen to prepare whatever kind of meat we planned to grill. He always showed up clean and happy, smelling of Zest soap. I wrestled with mixed feelings after realizing my dad evolved into a much better man than the one choked by the grip of being an attentive father to two young boys. But, hey, take good old-fashioned quality time when you can.

I got the sense he enjoyed being in the kitchen with his son, doctoring steaks for the grill. But of course, doing this each night, we also drank beer. A lot of beer. This regular practice made my life and our relationship a billion times less complicated. Lesson learned. To fabricate a dream dad, overhaul yourself into his favorite drinking buddy. Color me aware.

We kept the conversations light, never veering out of the topical safe lanes custom-built for distant relationships between men: sports, movies, and the weather. My dad persisted in being a Nebraska farm boy to the core. And I got a kick out of the visible amazement of him discussing California's exceptional climate. He often pointed out Santa Barbara's bizarre absence of mosquitoes —the menacing little bloodsuckers happy to stab us both like pincushions during summer visits to his farm.

"I mean, if I were a mosquito, I'd want to live here," he'd say.

On the odd occasions we ran low on topics to chew through,

Chick Hearn's voice filled the unwelcome void. My dad enjoyed listening to Laker games more on the radio than watching them play on TV. His insane choice to dismiss seeing Magic Johnson run Showtime's fast break validated my latent suspicions he's still loonier than a gypsy running Russian roulette contests out of a bowling alley basement. But after one quarter of listening to Chick's animated call of the game, I would've been fine never seeing another Laker game with my eyes. Unless they ever faced Michael Jordan's Bulls in the finals. A child and his silly dreams.

I enjoyed these nights with my dad more than a thousand backyard keg parties back home. Our mutual lack of interest in patching up old wounds to stitch a more traditional father-son relationship together became the highlight of the summer, if not my entire life.

My dad remarried. And I admired his second wife and enjoyed her company. She had a daughter from a previous marriage who was four years younger than me and owned a music collection, which made mine comparable to a Disney soundtrack. Being equally unselfish and hip, she made me copies of her progressive mix tapes delivering the best efforts of Jane's Addiction, Nine Inch Nails, and L.A. Guns.

I think his wife thought of me as a decent person too. But throughout the summer, I started sensing I represented a threat to her way of life. And I understood why. In most cases, houseguests age like fish, meaning the freshest company starts spoiling to rot after three days, four tops.

Knowing this, I absorbed the increasing frequency of her passive-aggressive observations and sarcastic quips at my expense, classifying them as nothing more than the friendly fire from a family warrior establishing clarity around the border. I silently vowed to fight alongside her to protect her turf and vision.

She and I never discussed the escalating effects caused by my prolonged presence, but I sensed the unspoken reasons why and where she landed on the matter of introducing physical reminders of the moody past into my dad's new and brighter way of moving through life.

I should've communicated my unwavering support as a comrade backing her right-minded cause. The lifestyle she served to protect was a living situation she willed into existence out of thin air. A miracle, in my estimation, to turn my dad into her world's primary source of love and warmth.

And during their six-month dating period, which culminated into a courthouse wedding, I maintained zero doubt she encountered a hot glimpse or two of the tortured man I remembered. I honored her commitment to protecting her turf as a battle-ready exercise to prevent seeing that wounded man again.

As a result, I represented a direct threat to peace by her estimations, like a delivery vehicle carrying enough reminiscent dynamite to flatten her world if my dad happened to light the fuse poking out from a single, explosive stick. Considering this, I signed on to support her mission the best way I reasoned possible —by minding my own damn business and keeping my mouth shut if ghosts from the "good ol' days" showed up unannounced, threatening to slither into our late-night conversations when we drank to excess.

But war tends to punish soldiers caught off guard, like when the undersized Greeks defeated the mighty Trojan army by harnessing the destructive might of an oversized wooden horse used to slip into Troy unnoticed. Somehow, in a blurry ruse, the memories shared between a father and son staged a similar attack, only instead of a horse, they poured out of a bottle of tequila and forever decimated my standing as a trusted partner in her mind.

I don't remember the night's conclusion or what we talked about that crossed the line. Only the last few shots of tequila we each threw back as sloppy aperitifs. I woke up early the next day hungover but determined to reach the golf course before the slow-playing retirees teed off and destroyed all hope for a round played in under six hours.

Despite the blurry way the night ended, my stepmom set up the coffee machine, and I rejoiced seeing a full pot steaming on the warmer. The digital clock said 6:30 a.m. Outside, the sky remained dark. But the pleasant tranquility forever connected to the salty air and fog typical of Santa Barbara mornings concealed itself behind a chilling mask.

Instead, I sensed a sinister presence, as if being studied from afar by a curious wolf or a vindictive spiritual being. But on the other hand, this was California. If anything scouted me through a window, it was likely a serial killer sitting in a stolen van across the street, waiting to skin me alive because he needed a new face to wear at Tai Chi class.

After the golf round, which I whizzed through in three hours, I drove down to State Street and ate a cheeseburger. I spent the next few hours nosing through a bookstore and got back to the house around three o'clock. The unmoving silence inside bothered me. Eerie and frigid, as comfortable to stand in as the lobby of a morgue.

An auspicious number of empty Coors beer bottles cluttered the kitchen counter, an unusual sight for several reasons. But the fact my stepmom's commitment to keeping a clean house exceeded every definition of compulsive madness stood out to me as the most peculiar.

My dad sat outside, alone on the porch, clutching a beer, and staring past the ocean at nothing. That or Neptune's horizon.

I recognized this departed gaze all too well from my childhood when my dad zoned out to conduct the same unsettling visual inventory of the unknown in the barbed minutes following another heated screaming match with my mom.

I grew to fear seeing this ominous expression more than the boogeyman sitting on my bed, sharpening his horizontal chopping ax against my baseball trophies. A shiver ran down my spine.

I stayed quiet and still. My dad, locked in his grim trance, remained oblivious to my whereabouts, and I intended to stay out of sight. So, I quietly shuffled the holy hell back. I rode the remainder of the sunny day out in my room, lying on my bed, imagining animal shapes forming in the ceiling's skim coat.

Over the next five days before my summer semester ended, we stopped cooking out. Instead, by choice, I ate dinner early and alone four times, and we slogged through a grueling family meal on my last night as their guest.

After I packed up my stuff, including my first college report card marked with two As, I tiptoed out to their porch with a six-pack of Coors and sat back in a lounge chair to celebrate my grades by getting tanked.

About an hour later, when I twisted the cap off my sixth beer, the buzzy stirrings of excitement about my immediate future showed up to endorse my assurances. I finished a solid trial run at the college level. And proved I bore the right stuff to go the distance. I also deduced with absolute clarity that California was no place for me to go about pursuing a purposeful future.

Besides, I missed my friends. And thinking about going to college together, the way we always talked about (two-day keg parties, boozy road trips, and an endless parade of college football games), reinforced my outlook like adding a steel beam.

I slipped into the kitchen to grab one more beer but first peeked in the bar cabinet, thrilled a bottle of tequila waited for me. I poured a quick glass and slammed it. The shot's heat warmed my insides and lightened the heft of concerns I dreaded dragging with me off to college.

I took another shot and then snatched one more beer. I stepped back out on the deck, stargazing, relieved my torpedoed idealism coasting toward college resurfaced like a burly life raft.

No care package stuffed with hunter green keepsakes from Dartmouth needed.

JIVEY LEAGUE
MATERIAL

Less than a week after fleeing Santa Barbara, I arrived in Norman, Oklahoma. Without the sedative benefits stemming from a full-frontal lobotomy, the sudden change in scenery did to my nervous system what ten gallons of vomit can do to a five-gallon urn.

But enrolling at the University of Oklahoma topped my new and improved list of sensible reasons to pursue higher education: to spite my father.

If you recall, my dad bleeds Nebraska red. An incurable disorder which goaded him to rank the Viet Cong guerrillas patrolling the Ho Chi Minh Trail as better folks than the criminals affiliated with Sooner football.

For this reason, enrolling at OU equipped me with a weaponized talking point, providing an immediate boost to the depleted emotional arsenal I depended on for protection during the dogfights specific to our fractured relationship's endless war. Arming me with counteroffensive firepower, topical and easy to deploy, perfect for neutralizing our combative phone conversations before things escalated. So instead of skirting calls, my refreshed battle plan called for deploying my college name into the phone's mouthpiece, audibly ramming the revolting words right up his ass.

Imagining our call on Thanksgiving, as the Sooners pistol-whipped his dumbstruck Cornhuskers like rural perverts caught groping sheep, filled my heart with festive warmth kindred to holiday blessings, gratitude, and blinding joy.

But because I spent the summer in California starring in an art-house production of *Father Knows Best on Acid*, I missed out on freshman orientation, making me the one student out of ten thousand who missed the campus tour, didn't register for a single class, and lacked an ID card, which administrators encouraged new students to always carry to avoid getting gunned down by a campus posse of Keystone Cops. However, I did manage to join a top fraternity.

I long aspired to be a part of all the brotherly hazing I learned about listening to stories told by my dad and the older guys I idolized from my high school. But in real life, soon, I found the rituals associated with pledgeship as proficient at undercutting my collected enthusiasm about college life as mystery meat served in the student cafeteria.

Whenever an active member bawled me out (often), my mind tended to wander off and deliberate over things like dinner, which girl to take on a date, and if the red-faced putz screaming in my face got tired of sizing his dick up to a crayon.

When I considered essential topics like this and thought about the million other activities happening on and around a college campus, opting in for a semester of fraternal abuse left me with a scorching case of buyer's remorse. And since the incessant chatterbox inside my head made all the obnoxious and nasty things these boys screamed at me sound like love-struck sonnets, their time got devalued too.

In less than a month, when I got comfortable using the campus map, I went straight to the registrar's office and dropped every class. Then I started sleeping until three in the afternoon, lacking the power needed to slide out of bed. A condition credited for pulling me down my first pit of depression, which only let up when my friends and I cracked open beers in the evening.

Speaking of depression, during this time, I packed on a startling amount of weight. But rather than buying a secondhand Mumu to screen my shame, an article of loose clothing worn by Oklahoma's hefty set with admirable nonchalance, I covered up my excess weight with the vilest variety of self-inflicting humor.

For example, before my buddies reamed me for the appalling amount of fried food piled on my tray or compared my new size to the campus bus, I launched into a monologue celebrating my dubious life as a whale beached in Oklahoma.

Can you believe this? I got a ticket for jogging topless by the same cop who let me off for speeding because I wasn't wearing a bra.

In October, I drove home for my birthday. (Yeah.) I told my mom I made a colossal mistake in picking a college and how I decided against returning. As always, my mom imparted her unconditional love and support. But she didn't express any shock or find my news the least bit surprising, which I found unsettling.

What I needed and wanted took shape as a reverential ass whipping. To get browbeaten to a pulp. For someone to smack my face and scream, *you're too damn good for this*, to *man up!* or *dare to dream!* and come carrying a kit to help patch the holes in my sinking raft.

However, I reasoned, anybody paying attention to my body of work over the past five years imparted justifiable cause to use their "win one for the Gipper" speech written for me to line their cat box.

In that case, the only pep talks came from my disgusted internal voice, which made Jimmy Stewart's rant in *Mr. Smith Goes to Washington* sound like the sweetest mom in Kentucky using sign language to tell her deaf son she wanted to rub his cookie-stuffed tummy.

After the holiday break, when my friends fled back to college, I hit rock bottom so hard the ground shook two towns over. And making my version of living hell hotter, my mom and stepdad happened to be the last people on earth without cable television. So, the only shows available for my viewing pleasure during the skittish weekday hours between 10:00 a.m. and 3:00 p.m. embodied programs attractive to advertisers keen on connecting with the biggest losers on earth.

The same ads ran every day in heavy rotation, created by sleazy lawyers, timeshare hustlers, and shifty peddlers selling miracle mops and spray-on hair. Without question, this constituted the time of day when Madison Avenue stopped working to empty their bowels.

My favorite spot promoted an unlicensed rehab facility. Their ad provided a pop quiz to help all the suicidal flameouts like me watching determine if the way we drank would soon kill us and everyone who loved us unless we dropped everything and checked into their facility—in the next ten minutes!

Of course, according to this quiz, if you drove past a Spuds Mackenzie billboard on your way to feed the homeless, you graded out as a degenerate alcoholic lucky to be alive. But from where I sat, I basked, proud to pass a test written to trick divorced fathers and pickled housewives. And to be honest, at the time, I stopped drinking. Not intentionally, more of a coincidence. My parents didn't keep liquor in the house, and I toiled through days too ashamed to show my face outside its walls.

After a week, seconds before my brain exploded, I quit watching television and started running. My chunky legs retained less bounce than wet garbage, and I found hauling my fat ass down one block less enjoyable than swimming through construction tar, but I forced myself to keep moving forward for two whopping miles, creating a scene recognizable to anyone familiar with Willem Dafoe's overdrawn death toward the end of *Platoon*.

When I finished the first run, I thought my heart might beat out of my ears. But nearing a breathless death, I managed to spin up the first positive thought about myself in months. So, I started running every morning.

My stepdad belonged to a swanky men's health club downtown. I fell into an energizing pattern of visiting this gym every night. First, I played hoops to warm up my body, followed by squeezing out the toxic demons acidifying inside my muscles by lifting weights and pulling on cables before letting a StairMaster administer the savage, hour-long beating I needed and deserved.

What I loved most about working out occurred afterward cleaning up. The water from this gym's showerheads burst out with the pressure of a water cannon used to put out city fires. And inside the stalls hung dispensers filled with fragrant soaps and shampoos, which I dutifully wasted obscene amounts of. As a result, when I left the gym each night, clearheaded and scrubbed cleaner than Howard Hughes's breakfast spoon, I trusted better days lay straight ahead.

Getting my body back in shape prompted me to start tuning up my brain. I grew up an avid but sporadic reader. If a story or subject caught my interest, I finished books straight through. And I typically went on a literary strike until another shiny topic sparked me into action. But now, I made an appointment to read for two uninterrupted hours each night before allowing myself to catch up on world news through Letterman's monologue.

Granted, this all went down before self-help books fell from the sky like wartime flyers over villages already bombed, so I stuck to mainly reading fiction. But I did start flipping through uplifting Horatio Alger-esque autobiographies at the bookstore to satisfy my newfound interest in what's humanly possible.

I picked up *Awaken the Giant Within* by Tony Robbins, an international bestseller validated by gushing celebrity sound bites on the back cover over Tony's magical framework for success.

After reading Tony's book, I know anything is possible, including winning the Super Bowl! boasted Jim Kelly.

I skimmed through the book. Twice. Failing both times to identify anything respective to Tony's metamorphic scheme to rouse anything inside me, much less an alleged giant. Mine must've been sucking on a King Kong–sized lollipop made of Rohypnol because I struggled to find a single line of directional truth in this hammy book awash in bald-faced lies.

One day, per the book, Tony lived in a seedy apartment and washed his dishes in the bathtub every night, whining like a newly kidnapped child about the total loser he grew up to be. But without an explanation—poof—Tony is traveling to deliver a keynote speech to the most significant business leaders and athletes on earth, flying in his private, pimped-out helicopter.

This exclusive event took place in Newport Beach. And as he helicoptered south from Calabasas, sneering down at the hapless idiots forced to drive cars through the hell of morning traffic inching down the 405, he took a moment to bask in how peachy his life became since the Jolly Green Giant within stopped catnapping in the pea garden.

Did I miss something? How exactly did Tony turn his miserable life around? I bet the man who wrote *Jacob's Ladder* is more confused than me by the baffling narrative gaps in Tony's rags-to-riches story. I chalked his inexplicable success up to America's overwhelming preference to inject snake oil into every problem to avoid the suffering coupled with hard work.

Not only that, but I'm sure his questionable ties to Scientology played a role. But unless I found myself scrubbing calcified SpaghettiOs off my only dinner plate with a toothbrush and bathwater, I planned on steering clear. Reciting alien chants and mud wrestling with Tom Cruise? There must be a better way.

Regardless, I continued ramping up my physical health and sanding down the idle knots rotting in my brain, reading the classics, and mixing in an occasional how-to book written by someone interested in doing more than blowing private helicopter smoke up my ass.

Nobody confused my pursuit to improve myself with Balboa's comeback montage in *Rocky II*, but I discovered infectious energy engaged in the requisite tasks. They were designed to tighten the essential springs proven throughout history to help weary burnouts bounce back from their prolonged visit to hell. Best described in Dana Plato's inspiring memoir *Look Out, World, Here I Come!*

But sprouting out of a broiling abyss didn't come cheap. So, I built my last objective around rebuilding the laughable balance in my checking account to finance my next getaway. I secured a paying job at a children's hospital through a temp agency. And as much as I appreciate your sensible instincts, no, my new role didn't require me to dress in a clown suit.

Instead, I served as the hospital's courier, a glorified errand boy. I drove a small truck around town to pick up or deliver various medical devices to different departments throughout the city's extensive hospital system. The job required little to no thought to complete the day's tasks. And I welcomed the long, solitary moments afforded to me wheeling around town in the delivery truck.

What I enjoyed most about the job came through connecting with other people working at the hospital. One guy, who became a regular lunch companion, spent forty-five years in the military. Now in his seventies, he drew a livable pension and did odd jobs at the hospital because his wife of fifty years cracked the whip anytime she found his feet on the coffee table.

At lunch, when he wasn't bragging how the thirty-year-old engine under the hood of his Buick didn't burn oil, he bellyached about the executive dopes turning the Texas Rangers baseball team into a national joke. Every boneheaded move they made, he cursed, they did to screw him.

We ate in the hospital cafeteria, which served an assortment of fresh foods. Being health focused, I loaded my tray up with foods deemed nutritious, starting with a generous scoop of rice, which I buried under a sloppy mess of pinto beans, along with a baked potato and a towering glass of orange juice.

One day, while gathering my winning lunch combo, a nurse standing next to me in line scoffed.

"If I cut in line, I apologize," I said.

"No, I'm confused by the food on your tray," the nurse replied.

She started pointing out the appalling percentages of starch-based foods I picked and offered to walk me back through the line and choose foods representing a more balanced and nutrient-rich lunch.

I invited her to join our table. Over the next half hour, she proceeded to tell us about the hidden evils embedded in starchy foods made up of complex carbohydrates and explained things like why people eat too many of them (because we're stupid) and how these dirty carbs caused the distressing obesity epidemic swallowing up our country.

She drilled into the shifty political interests propping up major food producers. These illicit partnerships gave food corporations unchecked authority to spin up outrageous lies about sugar and fat to ensure their scurrilous profits kept stacking through the clouds, allowing lobbyists to drag home trash bags full of cash. All siphoned from pocketbooks belonging to unwitting consumers and their hideous, potbellied children. This grave injustice inspired her to study nutrition in college and drove her to become a leading advocate in her field.

Throughout lunch, while she spoke, my cranky veteran buddy rolled his eyes, groaned, and huffed as she alleged Buick symbolized Detroit's incompetence or prattled on about the built-in advantages of being a communist. But to me, listening to her story made for a remarkable conversation.

The contagious way she spoke about her life's mission powered by a meaningful purpose forced me to think deeper into my plan. Or, I should say, create a plan. I couldn't help but hold this conversation up against my last ten thousand, which all centered around the number of kegs we floated at a party, the number of kegs needed for the next party, and why we never thought about renting a margarita machine until the final dark moments before passing out.

This lunchroom encounter inspired me to eat more vegetables and lean meats, sure. But it opened my eyes to the gifts perfect strangers were willing to give anyone interested in accepting them. To receive said offerings, infinite and always available, only required showing interest in another person's life and the facility to stop blabbing about yourself.

Of course, no sooner than I conceived this folksy notion celebrating the chatty genius inside all of us, my car's radiator sprung a leak, forcing me to call in a tow. I rode shotgun in the cab on the way to the repair shop. And as I listened to the tow truck driver nitpick over the stunts in *Point Break*, I found myself searching the truck's floors for brake fluid or motor oil—any fluid fatal enough for killing myself to prevent hearing more of his stupid thoughts.

Over the next four months, I continued popping out of bed each morning without an alarm, charging my batteries up with a clean and energizing power, getting more excited about the fall semester, and giving college another run, wherever that might be.

THE
SHAPES OF
WRATH

I grew up believing my grandfather, my dad's father, recognized his strength and toughness anytime *Mutual of Omaha's Wild Kingdom* featured a rhinoceros or a musk ox.

My first memory of Joe involved him chasing down a full-grown hog that poked through the pen. He picked up the squealing pig with bare hands and hurled the three-hundred-pound clump of ham back over the fence like the filthy beast weighed less than a beach ball filled with helium.

But in his sixties, a doctor delivered bad news: bone cancer. And his superhuman skeletal frame deteriorated overnight, crumbling faster than the chalky shell of a store-bought apple pie.

My temporary gig at the hospital ended. And I preferred not to stick around Fort Worth, suspecting (being positive) I might fall back into a routine propped up by bad habits the second my buddies got home for the summer. Plus, since my grandmother lived alone, I believed her appreciation for my company corresponded with mine regarding hers. So, I packed up and drove twelve hours to spend my summer with her at the farm.

Almost everyone in my life categorized me, fairly or not, as an introvert. Or, depending on who you ask, a brooding prick. But not her. She focused on people in a narrative sense, interested only in their evolving story instead of a label derived from past actions or hearsay. I never met anyone as wise or as determined to reside in the present moment. Moreover, she listened in a way which made me happy to talk.

She also loved cooking. Each day, she prepared and served three hearty meals made from scratch. We ate at a round table in front of a giant picture window with long views of their expansive farmland.

My newly acquired nutritional intelligence about the starchy evils lurking in certain foods made inhaling the stacks of fried chicken and piles of mashed potatoes she dished out every day for lunch tough on my resolve. But trying to explain the benefits of moderation to the town wino would take less time than addressing the delicate and self-absorbed reasons I waved off the gravy.

Besides, I had to consider my safety and well-being. It's possible walking my grandmother through my fussy preoccupations with food might prompt a reaction from her mirroring Kathy Bates's response to Jimmy Caan upon learning his character in *Misery* tried to escape.

Instead of letting the sight of her pants-popping dishes launch me into a dysphoric flight of psychotic rage, as Kate Moss does whenever she's offered a Tic Tac, I increased the mileage of my daily jogs to stay ahead of the girthy stampede.

My uncharted runs took me along winding dirt roads coursing through and around surrounding farms like a network of free-flowing veins. These roads got built to transport various forms of edible commerce from one place to another. So, whenever I jogged on these functional dirt roads for exercise, the grizzled farmers passing by on their John Deere tractors frowned at me, convinced I aspired to be a ballerina or smoked a ton of dope.

In less than a week, my grandmother and I got along like old friends. In the evening, we read books. She plowed through novels written by Sidney Sheldon and Danielle Steel. And I worked my way through paperbacks by Elmore Leonard, Pat Conroy, and Stephen King.

When I read everything in my stack, I grabbed her well-read copy of *The Other Side of Midnight* by Sidney Sheldon, and I found out fast why the man sold over three hundred million books worldwide. Sure, his sweeping, generational sagas vividly described dashing characters plotting their devious ways through the world's most exotic settings.

But I developed an opinion people paid for the astonishing number of steamy interludes between these characters occurring on every third page. These slippery scenes, penned with stimulating detail, made the explicit submissions slumming in the back pages of *Penthouse* less provocative than a celibate monk's grocery list.

I also got hooked on her favorite soap opera, *Days of Our Lives*, and made sure to be in the living room sitting next to her at 12:30 p.m. sharp. Of course, we cackled at the show's shameless overacting and were quick to point out each episode's most rueful moment, which always included the same character, who, for reasons unclear to everyone, including God, wore a pirate patch over his eye.

Often, later in the evening, our discussions pivoted to her son, my dad. She acknowledged and despised his demons. And knowing how the complicated relationship between her son and me unraveled weighed heavy on her maternal heart.

We discussed the previous summer when I lived with him in Santa Barbara. I kept the play-by-play positive, withholding the details around my dad's drastic shift in mood when his ghoulish memories came flooding out of the dark retrospective cracks in his battered brain. I grew too protective of both to dish frosty dirt.

And I suspected pointing out my dad's menacing behavioral ticks was unnecessary if not a self-serving insult to the depth of her observational intelligence on the matter. No different from someone new to golf describing the slope of the Old Course at St. Andrews to Jack Nicklaus.

One night, she pulled out the high school yearbook capturing my dad's senior year, and we flipped through the pages chronicling his bygone life together. I think she wanted me to absorb the permanent images of my dad as their small town's shiniest star. Or perhaps to prod herself of those times long forgotten.

My dad's senior portrait reminded me of a Hollywood headshot of a matinee idol. He projected an electric smile. And despite the bright shine coming out of his intelligent eyes, when I peered close enough into them, the conflicting intentions squabbling behind them stood out like the word "REDRUM" scribbled on a mirror with red lipstick, only more disturbing. Already, battle lines existed, separating seekers from destroyers. Accordingly, the forthcoming battles fought over the ideological dispute inside him would soon cause enough material damage to both sides, resulting in a crippling impasse ending in an all-out war.

This dignified but haunting portrait of my dad, taken around my same age, made me sad and anxious. More so, knowing six short years after grinning for the camera, a higher-ranking Marine shoved him out of an HU-1 helicopter into the dark green jungles of Vietnam with nothing to grasp but distant memories of a better time and an M16 with a full clip.

Each night, after my grandmother went to bed, never later than 9:00 p.m. on her wildest night, I headed down to their basement and my room. The basement also contained an office with an antique kneehole desk with an old typewriter sitting on its stained mahogany top. Next to the office, they built out an entertainment room, furnished with a black leather couch and television alongside a bar seldom used but well stocked.

As much as I enjoyed my grandmother's company, which I did more than anyone's, the inherent exhilaration spawned from sitting in front of the typewriter each night couldn't be beat.

Before I sat down, I poured myself a tall glass of whiskey at the bar. Next, I took a long, thoughtful stare at the blank piece of white paper hanging out of the typewriter, mesmerized by the imaginative thoughts and words sure to end up on the page.

Submerged in my most natural, free-flowing state, I wondered if Zen masters experienced something similar when they yammered on about roses in full bloom. Could it be I backslid into being the only person my age obsessed with answering pretentious and idiotic questions like this? And the only one plagued with uninterrupted frustration at how enlightened people willed this kind of exhilarated sensation into existence with less mental and physical effort than an everyday oddball like me put forth spreading peanut butter across a slice of bread?

Regardless of what hyperharmonious moments like this denoted or what caused them, I wanted to extend the duration of their stay anytime they came knocking on my door. And as I pecked at the keys on the typewriter writing the opening lines of the Great American novel, I discovered the elevated state I coordinated each night revealed itself halfway through my third glass of whiskey. I also realized these sensations tended to stick around as long I kept refilling my glass when empty.

When my summer on the farm came to an end, the idea of leaving saddened me. But I was ready to make a real run at college, better prepared than the blip before.

As I turned off the dirt road leading out of their farm and accelerated toward the paved highway somehow connected to home, I liked the places my life might go.

But with each full rotation of my forward spinning tires, the chasm between where this ambiguous place existed and the practical questions about reaching a comically undefined destination continued expanding like the size of Brendan Fraser's pants.

LOVE AT
FIRST BLIGHT

On the last day of the spring semester, after wrapping up my second uninterrupted year of college, I allowed my cagey self-esteem out for sunshine. After finding my stride in Austin, I stitched together another solid outing, wrestling in a set of decent grades bolstered by honest-to-goodness praise imparted on the creative papers I scribbled together and submitted. My buddies and I decided to round up some girlfriends of ours and celebrate our admirable efforts with an open-ended session of daytime drinking.

That's when I first laid eyes on the girl who forced me to reconsider the proposition I developed about marriage. A sweeping thesis hatched by observing my parents, which proposed wedlock as an arrangement couples entered only if their long-term intentions entailed the fixed delivery of searing pain to the other one's life.

"Who is she?" I asked.

My anxious sense of urgency demanded an answer right away, frightened she might vanish from the world at any second in an illuminated cloud of pixie dust. But instead, I fell into an unexpected trance. Made more unusual because, at the time, she wasn't soaping up a sporty red convertible and falling out of a string bikini, making the stretched nylon Bobbie Brown wore in Warrant's lewd video for "Cherry Pie" less titillating than an Irish chambermaid's dusting frock. Well, to be sure, she stood meddling next to a red convertible. A Pontiac Firebird. An automobile *MotorTrend* magazine hailed as a cure for zestful exuberance.

And instead of washing the red car, she demonstrated the process of coming unglued. Gracelessly cramming packed boxes into the insipid compact car's limited space and sweating buckets through her clothes—a simple outfit structured around rumpled khaki shorts from The Gap and a ratty, frat-party T-shirt. Two items of clothing, I thought, when paired together, are to happenstance arousal as a stained hotel duvet is to a beleaguered traveler's peace of mind.

Still, I pressed for an introduction. Finally, one of the girls with us called out her name, motioning her to come over to our car.

Her name was Lucia, and as she floated over, I tensed up, suddenly doubting the adequacy of my snappy and irreverent one-liners I usually discharged with the ease of turning a sink's tap.

The closer she got, the more hamstrung I became. Eerily similar to the customary stress-related nightmares prone to visit and hack through the silky webs failing to protect my peaceful sleep. Finding myself knee-deep in a soupy tar pit and sinking fast, screaming for help, only to realize my tongue turned into a gardening clog. This panic, I imagined, could only be appreciated by Ed McMahon if an unthinkable turn of events barred him from knocking back a fifth of Smirnoff before a taping of *The Tonight Show*.

My sudden inability to speak turned out to be a blessing because I sensed she distanced herself from flippant small talk. Moreover, I perceived her being a seeker of the unconventional. As a girl equipped with an infinite pool of depth who delighted in tossing ham-fisted gibber-jabber out with the morning trash.

Her sandy green eyes broadcast a deep sadness. But since the slightest sliver of light still fluttered behind them, I regarded her sour mood as fleeting. Speculating this, I thought saying something playful and sarcastic would make her smile. But I suspected anyone approaching her with a cheap laugh and bombed had a better chance of winning the lotto than getting a date with her. With my comedic chops under review, the risk associated with a crash and burn kept me from saying, "You look great. Headed to a formal?" Thank God.

I didn't meet her again until three months later when the fall semester started cranking back up. She starred in a sorority rush production. One of those variety shows put on to dazzle incoming first-year students into joining their tribe.

Don't scoff. By comparison, these productions differed from the aggravating theatrical belly flops exhibited on cruise ships or birthed during improvisational workshops tailored for corporate wonks. Think *Saturday Night Live*, excluding the year 1985, of course, when a vodka-soaked Anthony Michael Hall inexplicably joined the cast.

Unquestionably, these girls put in the concentrated time required to create a professional-grade show, as evidenced by the high level of craftsmanship all over the stage and in the programs. The performance imparted all the attributes of an old-time Broadway hit. Bursting with overblown song and dance numbers which rewarded attentive ears with inappropriate and pointed lyrics. And rolled out a parade of bloated caricatures walking off sky-high planks into boiling pools of toxic irony. All served up with a wicked, unapologetic level of haughty self-awareness, reminding me of the best work produced by Mel Brooks in his prime.

Moreover, the performance got boosted into the stratosphere by precise sequences of turbocharged choreography. The dance numbers utilized turned-in knees, sideways shuffling, and rolled shoulders in such an obsessively unflawed way, I wondered if the sorority girl in charge got conceived under a ballet bar. Maybe her mom, a stately blonde jewel, the pride of a legendary oil family, fled to New York in a rebellious fit one week before her wedding to the state's most conservative dope and spent three spirited days and nights getting every cell of her brain bonked out by Bob Fosse.

And my hunch about the latent shine simmering behind Lucia's eyes proved correct. Only nothing prepared me for the brightness which blinded everyone in attendance. She portrayed herself as larger than life. Grand and hilarious, able to make the crowd roar with delight at a stormy monologue or a pinpoint smirk. Her command of the stage electrified the room. And the power radiating from her showy performance compelled other girls onstage to rise like being hoisted up by hidden ropes.

She played her character, a hyperstereotyped sorority snob, to absolute perfection. Making this lippy brat better than Zeus at discharging contemptuous thunderbolts down from the sky, engulfing anyone she surmised as deserving to burn in instantaneous hellfire. And from the depraved viewpoint of her character, this included everyone.

But I picked up on a curious vibe. As she continued to inject an explosive, joyful menace into the role, I noticed a series of pulsating waves signaling friction generated from somewhere deep inside her heart.

I recognized her total absorption in the present moment but discerned an internal distraction, thought by me to be her secret participation in a grinding match of speed chess between this liberated caricature she portrayed and the restricted reality-smothering curious soul, calling attention to the straightforward fact most of the people in her life provided all the dubious inspiration she needed to bring this magically rotten character screaming to life.

Unquestionably, on paper, the skit's prevailing motivation centered around getting laughs. But Lucia used her performance like a weapon, obliterating the restrictive life she enlisted into, coaxed by traditional pressures, as happy now as a falcon peering up at unbounded skies through the metal wiring of a parakeet's cage.

My life depended on making a connection. Plus, separated from the sweaty slog of jamming all she owned into a red Pontiac and demonstrating the same unruffled touch of a grizzled lumberjack jamming sequoia logs into the back of a Volkswagen, Lucia transformed into a creature a blind man could see was smoking hot.

Our first date couldn't be ordinary. Another forgettable dinner at a hapless chain restaurant like Chili's followed by enduring a brain-dead rom-com featuring Meg Ryan, Julia Roberts, or God forbid, the bumbling British jackass, Hugh Grant, playing a bumbling British jackass. So, I planned our first date around hitting a respectable band's weekly gig at a legitimate hole-in-the-wall music club on Sixth Street.

Before the show, we went to a bar near campus, and I ordered a pitcher of beer. She took a sip and grimaced. Seeing her discomfort, I offered to order wine. She said she liked the beer and only hated its lingering aftertaste.

"Well, um. Beer tastes different sometimes," I stammered.

In the brief silence following my boneheaded decree, I figured I lost her forever. Another one of my life's great "check please" moments. But soon, we entered deep conversations which picked up steam before busting through our personal boundaries with captivating disregard.

We shared and discussed our most unseen peculiarities and egregious misgivings at a comfort level unfamiliar to me before when speaking with anyone, including myself in front of a mirror or on long drives headed nowhere.

Indeed, as the intimate night went on, I cringed, thinking our paths crossed too soon, well before the point in my life when I imagined myself willing or capable of taking one step toward the serious business of growing up. I perceived the interconnected permanence accompanying true love, which is recognized as such only once over anyone's entire life on earth (if they're lucky), towered over my ramshackle ability to handle it.

The scientific accuracy of this self-assessment crushed me. So, after our two kindred souls smashed into each other, setting off a chain of events igniting the mutual creation of a transcendent and divine electromagnetic eruption of love, light, and bliss, all I hoped for was our night together ending with a memorable kiss.

And it did. Happening under a sudden, unexpected flash of a christening rain, no less.

GUESS WHO'S
NUMBING TO
DINNER

O ver the next three months, after our kiss, I lived in a
dreamlike state. I feared, at this point, saying I loved
her. But when I went home to Fort Worth for Thanksgiving break
while she headed south to San Antonio, my mushy, vulnerable
heart turned to stone. This minted our first experience in dealing
with the dreary torment of physical separation, bolstered by a
regional distance of only 250 miles, made to register in my lonely
mind as a billion.

She invited me to San Antonio the Saturday after Thanksgiving for a visit. And of course, to roll me out in front of her parents for a thorough inspection. The way a cart carrying raw cuts of prime beef gets paraded in front of discerning diners at an upscale steakhouse.

The drive from Fort Worth to San Antonio takes four hours. A straight shot down, north to south, on an interstate built for speed. A cakewalk of a drive I could complete wearing a blindfold and one I planned to start Saturday morning before sunrise.

On the Friday following Thanksgiving, I hit the town with my buddies one last time before we scampered back to the various college campuses to continue meddling in average work. The night began with no specific agenda. So accordingly, we drank like rodeo clowns honoring a fallen colleague's grisly on-the-job death. Our brotherly enthusiasm prompted us to create personalized living portraits glorifying the early stages of full-blown alcoholism. Unfortunately, this artistic twist inspired us to drink well past four in the morning.

I grew up reading *The Guinness Book of World Records*, getting a fresh new edition every year as a predictable but appreciated Christmas stocking stuffer from my grandparents. Off the top of my head, I can't recite the record for most Marlboro Lights smoked in one sitting by a nonsmoker, but I'm convinced I shattered the mark. Coincidently, I broke a few more records during that night, unofficially of course.

- The number of times the Cult's song "Love Removal Machine" was restarted to hear the opening riff.
- Consecutive stories starting with "Remember when that idiot…"
- Amount of beer spit out of a mouth due to uncontrollable laughter.

I snoozed through my alarm, which started beeping at five in the morning. Then I jerked awake at 7:30 a.m. to a gruesome jolt like a gorilla was stomping on my heart. It took more than a minute to engage my bearings and more time to stop being sure I had mutated overnight into a bullfrog, now afloat in a jar filled with formaldehyde.

Thirty minutes into the four-hour drive, my tart buzz disappeared, making room for the beastly hangover I deserved. Soon, despite slurping up a drum full of black coffee, playing *Love Removal Machine* at full blast, and choking down two Marlboro Lights I picked off the floorboard, I struggled to keep my eyes open.

In hindsight, if the opening sequence of *Meet the Parents* started this way, Greg Focker would hold a darker edge, giving Ben Stiller more to do than bark for mackerel like a showboating seal at SeaWorld. Considering this, he might've won an Oscar. Coincidentally, the degree of acting I needed to master in the next three hours.

The sun's blinding light and the endless, miserable road ahead forced me to pull over in Hillsboro and into a gas station, hoping for a miracle recovery. When my fairy-tale bounce back didn't happen, I scrubbed my face with powdered soap and bought a pair of cheap sunglasses along with a six-pack of Miller Lite.

Four hours later, I pulled up to Lucia's house, elated every cop in the state didn't join me. She stood outside their house, more of an estate, waiting for me. Somehow, in less than four days, she did the impossible and became more beautiful. A humbled lump in my throat stopped me from breathing. I didn't realize a person could rattle my heart this way.

I got out of my car. We crossed the ground between us and crashed into each other's arms. I squeezed her tight, smelling her hair, savoring her warmth, and basked in the miracle of her pulling me back.

But the dreamy fog safeguarding our embrace lifted fast, giving me an unsettling glimpse of my waking reality's actual whereabouts. I might as well have been sitting in front of a grinning cop, under an interrogation lamp bright enough to be seen from Mars, like the forces of my egregious decisions finally caught up to me, capturing me dead to rights, leaving me no choice but to blabber a full confession.

Yes, Officer, I agree a negative outcome of this meeting would ruin each subsequent second of my life. But, um, unfortunately, Officer, before coming, I drank more than Ted Kennedy at Easter brunch.

I learned her parents were lovely people and permanent fixtures on the South Texas social circuit from Lucia's friends. This is an unending series of extravagant parties thrown by dashing people who controlled every transaction in the southern hemisphere.

Families from Monterey powered by mysterious sources of breath-taking income. The oil and gas titans whose last names regularly appear in places like the front page of the *Wall Street Journal* and above museum doors. All rounded out with quirky hobbyists who filled their time hosting fundraisers, African trophy hunting, and acquiring priceless works of art the way most people collect matchbooks from their favorite dive bars.

These remarkable and wealthy people represented their peers, the distinctive and vibrant set of world-beaters they broke bread with. And up to this point, frankly, I never considered what her parents might think about me and my unremarkable story in comparison.

For starters, I was born outside state lines, in California no less. Universally, people from Texas viewed this as an irredeemable sin. No different from attending the University of Oklahoma, treating horses with indifference, or being open to adding common-sense measures to the Second Amendment.

Worse, out of the million movies I grew up watching, somehow I missed freaking *Giant*. So, regarding Texas lore and mystique, the only tangible thing I brought to the party took shape in the last few hours of Janis Joplin's life.

Walking into her house, I bit my lower lip to help keep my mouth shut. Lucky for me, her dad sucked all the air out of the room the second he trotted in. He had a substantial build paired with a sophisticated ruggedness which should've intimidated me to the point of running and screaming toward the front door.

But his chummy vibes transmitted a calming effect. The way the kick of a bass drum can steady a band's nerves before a gig. In my world, he appeared wildly overdressed for a Saturday afternoon. Million-dollar boots, custom trousers, and a pressed cotton oxford shirt. Plus, a gold nugget buckle stitched to the front of a full-grain leather belt worth more than my car. But he moved with the comfort and unrestricted ease of a single mom reheating last week's spaghetti in a terrycloth robe.

He also possessed a majestic dirty-blond handlebar mustache, making this the first handlebar mustache not freezing me to wonder about the meandering sequence of bad ideas which led an able man to think growing a crooked stripe of chintzy fuzz under his nose might shift Lady Luck's gaze his way. When we shook hands, the measured pressure in his grip implied his appreciation for how I treated his daughter, and I might be wise to stay the course.

He got tipped off I loved red wine. And the sight of two uncorked bottles breathing on the counter gave me hope for a second wind. He grabbed a bottle and filled two oversized, long-stemmed crystal wine glasses to the rim. Right away, I liked him.

Incidentally, her dad turned out to be a gifted and enthusiastic storyteller. And since my ability to speak a simple sentence got left somewhere between Waco and Austin, perhaps Lady Luck herself saved me from having to utter one drunken word.

With a booming voice and contagious zeal, one of the stories he told took place back in the '80s, back when everyone in Texas was swimming in cash. He and his wife, plus three other couples, decided on a whim to book a last-minute cruise on the QE2 bound for England for the tennis matches at Wimbledon. After six boozy nights on the ship, which required the men to wear black ties, they sailed into Southampton.

A month before, one of his friends sold his company for a small fortune and bought them privileged event badges, giving them full access to NBC's VIP tent. Once inside the tent, the champagne flood started flowing. After a few hours of heavy drinking, they got up and headed toward their prime seats at Centre Court, but not before bumping into the king of late night, the ultraprivate Johnny Carson. Starstruck, he approached Johnny and gave him a hearty Texas bear hug.

We think you're doing a fantastic job with the show in San Antonio, Johnny.

Johnny didn't say a word, and a rumor surfaced later Johnny's people raced him to the airport in an ambulance and flew him home to Malibu less than ten seconds after this personally harrowing encounter.

When Lucia's mom came down the stairs dressed for dinner, I almost spit out a mouthful of wine. She viewed the world through a set of stunning crystal blue eyes. More affecting than a mountain sky beaming with sunshine moments after a purifying shower of rain got pushed out by a strong gust of crisp wind, making the spectacular jewels hanging around her neck all but vanish.

The way I see it, nothing is less attractive than beauty held captive by a stingy, frigid owner who shares her gift only when its inconsiderate purposes are served. But she encouraged her ravishing attractiveness to run free, with benevolence, making it available to everyday dopes still seeking reasons to believe in careless dreams.

I appreciated this quality since the foundational layers propping up my own aspirations tended to melt faster than plastic soldiers in a psychotic child's microwave. As a result of meeting her, I experienced dramatic upticks in my self-worth, which I cashed in as a hedge to steady myself.

Hours later, at dinner, I made a silent vow to slow down with the drinks. Looking back, I should've stated my advice louder. Because somehow, all I kept hearing was a line said in the book *On the Road* by Jack Kerouac. When one of the characters, either Sal or Dean, screams like a blissful idiot, "You can't fall off a mountain!" Inspired by literary fact, as her dad ordered two bottles of wine, I asked for a gin martini.

I left San Antonio satisfied with my first impression. In short, I came across as witty and loving, backed by a confident humility, and buttressed with a gift for gab and a better-than-average visual appeal. No doubt I adored her parents. And if I had to guess, the adoration was mutual.

Given these reflections, imagine my surprise a few days later when I learned how the dinner went in real life. As Lucia ran down the play-by-play, the shame eviscerating my insides to soot burned so hot I almost screamed.

"I said what?" I asked over a hundred times.

In the end, apparently, I would've improved my initial impression by blowing our waiter for coke while maintaining direct eye contact with her dad.

Two weeks later, I met up with her parents, immediately launching into my *Guinness Book of World Records* attempt at history's most heartfelt, sincere, and woebegone apology for atrocious behavior delivered by a prick undeserving of God's grace.

Her dad thought the night turned out to be a hoot and reminded those present he could still outdrink a college man. And her mom blamed the whole night on him, giving me an inexplicable out, displaying a grace I never witnessed in humans before and haven't been privy to since. I'd grown so accustomed to fighting through life alone, the appropriate response to finding someone crouched in my corner holding a spit bucket and gauze eluded me, especially a woman of her esteemed caliber.

Lucia kind of laughed along, guarded, exercising adequate caution, but I interpreted that the severity of the situation pierced her heart with a hook. In less than three months of dating, she observed me flying off the tracks four times, with the worst crash occurring during an introductory dinner with her parents.

A few years later, her mom and I discussed the visit. At the time, the loving relationship between Lucia and me diminished down to the original romantic blueprints. The remainder of what we shared in the past or might in the future continued living off in a dark room, comatose, aided by sponge baths and a life support machine designed for blue whales.

She had already moved to San Francisco, and my pilgrimage

to New York was only weeks away. We still loved each other. A great deal, in fact. But not enough to travel over three thousand miles of lingering doubt.

Before my first visit, her mom told me she'd never seen her daughter in so much love. This terrified her because she couldn't handle her daughter's heart getting crushed. But when I met Lucia in their front yard, and we rushed into our long, sweet embrace, she spied on us from an upstairs window and said she loved me like her own from the tender way I held her daughter.

She added that if Lucia and I decided to pull the cord on our withering love, she wanted to remain friends with me for life. And she promised a future filled with catch-up lunches whenever she visited New York. Nothing anybody ever said to me challenged my longstanding belief that I was broken, doomed, and making a mess out of borrowed time.

As much as I hated the self-doubting bum who appeared each morning when I glanced in the mirror, her words gave me a reason to pause. If anything, now, going forward, whenever I hit rock bottom (a biweekly occurrence), I could utilize this memory the same way construction cleanup crews leverage lifting tongs and yank my body out of whatever dark hole or metaphorical gutter I plunged into the night before.

Because if a person of her character and pedigree found something sound and decent in me, in my worst condition, I might one day fool myself into thinking I differed from the horrible person I believed myself to be. Or so I hoped.

THE WEDDING
INCEPTION

During my final semester of college, I took a survey course examining the Great Depression. If I worked with a shrink at the time, the subconscious reasons I enrolled in a class exploring the severe desperation and misery responsible for ripping the hope out of 120 million people would've taken years to unpack, much less examine and make use of.

Of course, looking back, any Freudian flunky smoking a pipe and wearing round glasses could sniff out my self-destructive, neurotic motives with the ease of a black bear smelling a distant camper's hot-dog burp.

During the semester, I learned the Hoover Dam represents one of the seven wonders of the industrial world. But unfortunately, the construction of the engineering marvel took place during the Great Depression. Meaning all the dirty work hinged on the backs of displaced men with no choice in the matter since the merrymaking traders on Wall Street crushed their dreams like still glowing cigar butts tossed on a sidewalk.

Throughout the dam's chaotic five-year build, gruesome construction accidents killed thousands of men. So, it's fair thinking the horrid physical outcomes realized from these bumbling snafus made whatever ghoulish hell the trench fighters took in during World War I look like pinup posters of Shirley Temple licking a lollipop.

And the lucky men who didn't die got served rat stew and dirt biscuits for dinner and took regular lashes across the face administered by a foreman's trusty horsewhip if they so much as asked for salt. In the end, since everyone involved in the Hoover Dam's five-year construction project got railed by the government's bloodthirsty gang of financial goons, not a single man left Nevada with enough money to hoist his bones off the ground.

Not surprisingly, this triggered a considerable uptick in suicides and bumped up the country's murder rate tenfold. Worst of all, throughout the carnage, nobody exhibited the brainpower on par with Forrest Gump, who at least conjured up an idea for a wealth-creating bumper sticker after jogging through a pile of dog shit. Indeed, mistakes were made.

Keg parties aside, the approximation between the Hoover Dam's construction and my own five-year slog through college shared striking similarities, making me wonder what the surviving men did to celebrate once the project wrapped up.

In the wake of these interchangeable experiences, after Uncle Sam burned the festering labor camps to ash and flew home ticketed in first class, the total sum of their self-worth hovered below the accumulated matter steaming inside the site's busiest outhouse, assuming their sentiment matched mine, of course.

From there, I bet they packed up their hobo sacks and jumped on the first boxcar headed east, toward the lonely nothingness of their botched destinies. Similarly, I snagged a twelve-pack of Coors Light and scurried home to drink alone in the dark. I played NHL '94 on Sega while second-guessing every decision I ever made.

The same week before I graduated, my brother married his college sweetheart. If a more perfect match for my brother existed on earth, she kept herself well hidden. With no plans to celebrate my trifling graduation, I intended on using a few quiet minutes alone during the reception to acknowledge the accomplishment by slugging down a tequila shot and a beer.

Overall, I deemed my life inconsequential but manageable. The only cause for concern came from the looming, obligatory multiday encounter with my dad over the wedding weekend. The last time we spent time together happened over a year ago, and we spoke on the phone at the same rate as snow blizzards crippled Austin.

Fifteen months earlier, my brother and I received a bizarre message from my dad. After missing out on the better part of my life and letting me plot my own way across the minefields leading to manhood (forced weekly phone conversations notwithstanding), he decided my brother and I deserved the gift of his full, devoted attention. Of course, we both received this news the same way a pastry chef might if the dishwasher popped into the kitchen offering tips to improve the macarons.

Without exception, my dad's perverse indulgence to transform himself into a real-life Mike Brady coincided with receiving a plastic chip from his program, indicating he stitched together a streak lasting six months without getting sloshed. As an encore, he believed starting a business would bring us together and make up for all the time he pissed away regarding us.

He rambled on about buying an apartment building in Austin to renovate and manage together. Meanwhile, all I talked about over the last five years (when we did talk) swirled around moving to New York the second I finished college. Once he realized my brother and I lived busy lives of our own construction, his interest in being our dad lost traction sooner than I expected. And my expectations measured in hours.

So, after a few awkward dad moments (like when he compared his experience in Vietnam with Lucia's, who partied her way through Hanoi while taking a semester at sea), he packed up and hauled the sparse remains of his life back to California.

The weekend of my brother's wedding, my dad found himself

in fine spirits. At the rehearsal dinner, he gave a thoughtful, appropriate toast. He didn't use the occasion to make up for thirty lost years, and I admired his composed commitment to playing the moment straight down the middle.

Throughout both nights, his hands shook as if clamped to a pneumatic paint shaker. I sensed he found the weight of his self-awareness and how his life turned out crushing. From personal experience, I grasped the intensity at which his thirsty nerves were needling him to slam a quick drink. Watching him, I wondered where the best version of him would be in the alternate universe where he quit drinking the day after the *Cosmos* incident. What incredible accomplishments resided in a world where my family of origin stuck together and burst through life's restrictive barriers by being active and loving participants in each other's lives? Happy, joyful, and as tightly knit as the sheep's wool in a sturdy British peacoat.

After the wedding, we moved over to a lively reception with plenty of booze. Usually, at weddings (and funerals or on Tuesday nights), I drank like a fish. Instead, with my dad in tow, I sipped on an occasional beer, which he appreciated. Typically, my dad avoided joyful occasions the way longer-living bass swim past spinning hooks. Many times, I caught him lost in thought, staring out into deep space. Sometimes, his face contorted, suggestive of a formidable gloom, like the results came back from the lab, confirming the worst.

Of course, the hired DJ might've been spinning "Brick House" by the Commodores. A song notorious for making all reasonable people at weddings present themselves like they're grappling with lousy news.

When the wedding wrapped up, I dropped my dad off at his hotel. We shared a frozen moment between him getting out of the car and shutting the door. I considered parking the car and joining him in the lobby. Or asking the front desk for a cot to spend the night in his room. But the thought of sharing a room with my dad magnified our unsettling dysfunction, and I believed he thought the same.

After all these years, here we both stood on the same part of the beach looking out at the dangerous emotional breakers rolling into shore. In silence, we shrewdly communicated back and forth that no father and son had any business paddling into sentimental surf unless they believed in each other's ability to ride these dicey waves back to the sand unharmed. I imagined the two of us wading in the ocean's shallow foam. Father and son both void of expression, as if lobotomized, our unfocused eyeballs gawking at the miraculous waves created by God for us to ride in together, each holding a surfboard made from Popsicle sticks and rubber glue. At this point, I decided to head home.

The next day, I picked him up. To kill time before his afternoon flight, we camped out for lunch at a burger spot famous for serving thirty types of beer on tap, taking seats in front of a football game playing on the pub's oversized TV.

"You can get a beer. I don't mind," he spoke.

"I'm good. I don't want one."

A true statement. Because I didn't want one. I wanted six thousand. But I followed his lead and ordered a Coke. From his brooding mood, I decoded his endorsement in my conviction these edgy hours spent together would last forever.

We talked but didn't say much. I wished we could split a pitcher of beer, and I'm sure he thought the same. Drinking like we drank on my visits to California had a way of loosening the knots clotting our relationship. Temporarily, at least. Long enough to acknowledge, for better or worse, we shared the same blood.

I drove him to the airport and headed toward the parking lot since, back in the day, people parked their cars and walked ticketed passengers all the way to the gate. I preferred licking the bottom side of a toilet's lid over following him in but thought escorting him to the gate constituted the right thing for a son to do. For similar reasons, he insisted on getting dropped off at the curb. The mutual agreement to a quick goodbye relieved both of us, as evidenced by the matching deep releases of pent-up air.

When I stopped, he gathered his things and exited the car. I got out and gave him a hug. He hugged me back tight and sighed.

"I can't wait to get home," he said.

He made it halfway to the airport door and turned around. He wore jeans and a brown leather bomber jacket made for men much smaller, which didn't make him look cool, only uncomfortable. After offering me a half salute and a final wave, he smiled and shrugged, communicating the depth of understanding at his disposal on the matter of his life being a total wreck.

"Hey, at least I'm not flying to Cleveland," he said.

My dad's masterful knack for finding beautiful humor in life's ugliest moments empowered me to smile him away. I loved him dearly because of this. Despite the dark tension smothering out the best of us, he would always be the funniest man my good luck allowed me the pleasure of knowing.

Before he turned to leave, I recognized a speckled flash of youthful vigor on his face, reminding me of the portraits I studied flipping through his high school yearbooks at his farm in Palisade. But the innocence vanished sooner than it appeared. Now he resembled himself again, only much older, not as wise, and perpetually spooked.

He walked through the sliding doors into the airport, and I drove off. Saddened, but not at all surprised, at the toxic shape our synthetic relationship evolved into.

START
SPREADING
THE BOOZE

At the age of fourteen, many kids my age discovered troves of directional behavior to model their futures around leaking out of the one-dimensional teenagers portrayed on sitcoms like *The Cosby Show* and *Growing Pains* like fatal, odorless gas.

On the other hand, the functional blueprint resonating most with me drew the bulk of its inspiration from the ebb and flow of Michael Steadman's life, the charming but embattled lead character on ABC's critically acclaimed but mostly ignored show *Thirtysomething*.

Michael worked as a creative director employed by the city's most cutting-edge advertising agency. He fit the description of a contemplative if not a reluctant yuppie, and each week, his earthy idealism got sawed in half by his boss—a maniacal sociopath played by the slimiest creep ever yanked from central casting—or his frigid, unfeeling wife, who spent her days glaring at unpaid bills, guzzling white wine, and submerging under milky bathwater to practice screaming, "What's not to love?"

I raced out and bought the show's soundtrack. An exhilarating celebration of the flute's uncanny ability to ram a railroad tie through the display glass protecting overwrought emotions.

And each Tuesday night, inspired by the hopeful notes blowing out of Snuffy Walden's silver nickel flute, the accidental idea of becoming a deep-suffering ad man grew more and more into a dream worth chasing. Only not to Philadelphia.

Three weeks after my brother's wedding and two days before the world turned 1996, I hopped on a plane and flew to New York City with the express purpose of making my mark.

At the same time, the responsibility of keeping the cultural torch lit shifted to Generation X, and the idea of sitting on the bench as my people rewrote the world's story made me twitch with familiar regret.

After all, my roiled brain carted around the same cynical payload as my influential brothers and sisters. And they cashed in, dumping our generation's angry, disenfranchised, and sometimes ironic content into media outlets strangling the hope out of every person on the globe.

I generated plenty of crackerjack thoughts optimized to celebrate and intensify my generation's gloomy mood and reasoned that the most effective platform to broadcast my despondent ideals resided in printed magazines. Using obtuse headlines and shrill copy extolling the benefits of prescription-strength laxatives, cat box litter, and a specialized ironing starch geared toward hypermasculine Wall Street goons: *She'll Love How It Stays Stiff All Night.*

Not counting a bottle of Chivas (a gift) and a delusional pipe dream, I set off for New York carrying only two things: my advertising portfolio and an oversized gym bag stuffed with clothes best described playing a make-believe game of Jeopardy.

I'll take Manhattan Matters for $200.

The answer is, Seeing Jason's clothes.

What sent Anna Wintour into cardiac arrest?

Correct. We would've also accepted, what makes E's Fashion Police *hate men wearing hockey jerseys less?*

To commemorate my bold move, I polished off four beers followed by two double-Jack-and-Cokes on the flight. When I walked off the plane in Newark, I made a mad dash to the airport restroom. Refreshed, I headed to the luggage carousel, grabbed my bag, and walked to the cab stand, where I stood in the back of a line ten miles long.

Being late December, the temperature hovered between single digits. I buttoned up the only jacket I owned to no effect since the coat's manufacturer designed the flimsy garment for middle-aged hippies to keep handy if the temperatures at a bluegrass concert above Stinson Beach trickled below fifty degrees.

Fortunately, being half drunk dulled the pain of winter's bite. But I did perceive a chilling sensation of sorts, more associated with significant loss than the weather. A sharp shiver carved down my spine.

I checked for my wallet. All fine. My eyes darted down to my bag. Check. Not that the belongings inside introduced any risk of theft. I swallowed my heart, scanning every inch of surrounding space but failed to spot the one thing I feared went missing. My heart stopped.

I jumped out of the line and streaked inside. Being pre-9/11, before security required the signing over of a passenger's child to reenter an airport's terminal, nobody cared when I hurdled through the checkpoint with my hair on fire. I started at baggage claim, retracing every step from when I staggered off the plane and made a mad dash to the men's room. Where, if memory serves (a coin toss), I hung my book on the coat hook inside the stall I used.

The stall in the bathroom where I prayed my book hung hosted a wheezing guest. So instead of banging on the stall's door and having the most bizarre exchange of words between two humans since we stopped communicating with crude gestures and grunts (or getting my ass kicked), I patiently waited for the toilet's industrial-strength flush.

When the man pushed the door open, I rejoiced, seeing my book hanging from the hook drilled into the metal door.

Back in business and too relieved to consider the prognostic symbolism of the man's waste still circling in the toilet, impervious to the toilet's mighty pull, which, in hindsight, foreshadowed the ending of my New York adventure with all the nuance and subtlety of a homeless junkie banging a street sign with a walker pulled from a dumpster.

A month earlier, I found a room to rent in the back pages of the *Village Voice*. For New York, the monthly rate translated into an economic miracle compared with my sky-high expectations, especially for an apartment on the swanky Upper West Side.

Unbelieving, I called to verify the bargain-basement price and secured the place right away. And despite not understanding any of the muffled grunts coming from the stranger on the other end of the line, I applauded my shrewd thriftiness and considered the task complete.

I brimmed, marveling how I locked up a home in New York located in the same neighborhood as Sean Penn and Madonna, according to Charlie Sheen's real estate agent in *Wall Street*, at least. Never mind, a delusional fan murdered John Lennon in cold blood a few blocks over.

As the cab chugged its way up north through the snow and sludge jamming up the avenue, people on the street whisked along, dropping into shops, ducking into restaurants, and streaming in and out of Barnes & Noble, carrying books and coffee. Everybody wore fashionable clothes as if headed to a swanky cocktail party or holding tickets to a sold-out show at Lincoln Center.

These dashing and brave people represented the real New Yorkers, and I relished being their new peer and anticipated the day we all became inseparable friends. I continued ogling them with spellbound admiration, like a starry-eyed Wisconsin dope riding the tram at Disney World for the first time.

As we continued north, the clusters of beautiful people, I noted, began thinning out. And in another two city blocks, they all but vanished. The cab zoomed through the intersection at 90th, showing no signs of slowing down. Except for panhandlers, probable drug dealers, and the occasional washing machine box converted into a makeshift home, the streets showed no signs of life.

The cab made a sharp right turn on 104th and locked up the brakes, stopping in front of a nondescript brick building without an awning or a sign. Instead of a well-polished doorman guarding the door, greeting comers and goers with a pat on the back and a hokey quip about politics or the weather, a pile of garbage obscured a wooden entryway looking more like an inlet to hell.

Perhaps the cab driver stopped here to score a quick dime bag of gritty heroin and pick up a homeless prostitute for the ride home. At least I hoped so. Because if this building constituted my new home, any chance of me surviving the night probably rested on quick and easy access to both heroin and prostitutes.

I walked in, more confused than terrified. The lobby's dark walls, sketchy lights, and a twitchy odor—smoke blended with synthetic pine—did little to clear my spinning head.

I dragged my stuff to the front desk and, with each step, became more uncomfortable with how my frumpy clothes made me appear overdressed, as conspicuous as a careless man waltzing through a federal prison adorned in a black Kiton tuxedo.

The clerk standing behind the desk chewed on a wet cigar, squinting down at the pages in a notebook. Without looking up, he greeted me in a Russian accent. This did little to ease my concerns. Point-blank, I unwittingly entered either the lobby of an Armenian brothel or the set of a snuff film, forcibly cast to play the leading man.

Before drawing a conclusion, three girls around my age trotted down the stairs. They appeared to be happy and spoke with cheery British accents. But most importantly, they breezed by me and walked out the front door of their own free will. I almost dropped to my knees and wept with relief.

I paid a month's rent up front and got the key to my room, located on the first floor. At this point, I didn't expect to confuse my room with one at the Ritz, figuring the overall motif inspiring the decor came from an examination room at a free clinic or the front office at a prison.

But my aggressively low expectations about the room turned out to be much too high. Although, the room did boast a window covered by iron bars, providing guests with a unique street-level view of the happenings outside. Soon, the gritty sounds of the city's underbelly poured into the room. Sirens, engines, loud voices. No bloody screams followed by gunshots, though. But the night was young.

The feature my room lacked, however, potentially made everything up to this point child's play. I triple-checked. But the mission-critical lifestyle component I combed the room for in a panic didn't exist. And when I picked up a mysterious key off the bedside table chained to a small plastic sign, my worst fears came roaring to life.

"First-floor bathroom," I read out loud.

With nothing left, I collapsed onto the bed like a debt collector working for the mob cracked the back of my skull with a baseball bat. But the mattress made cheap springy sounds, recalling unwelcome images nobody deserved associating to a transient bed. I sat back up. A garish quilt and flat pillow covered the sheets. Knowing the amount of electroshock therapy needed to wipe my brain clean of seeing the sheet's troubling rips and splotches might kill me, I didn't pull the covering back. Not an inch. And I crashed back down and slept, fully clothed, for the next seventeen hours.

Despite my less-than-optimal living conditions, I woke up charged on the first Monday in January. And after taking the fastest shower of my life in the communal bathroom, I dressed for the battle of attacking New York. Outfitted in clothes made to protect brave men from the wrath of a gentle spring breeze, I left my room and marched to the subway, braving the same kind of icy winds endured by the doomed characters in the movie *Alive*.

I understood the advertising industry worked like a restricted club. Without an Ivy League degree or a blood relative with a black book filled with industry heavyweights weighing more than a box of Clio's, the odds of landing a job in advertising, especially in creative, were worse than Pauly Shore being knighted by the Queen of England.

To stand out, I had to demonstrate the grit and hustle lacking in the prep school Rohypnol dispensers competing for the same job. So, I strolled into the lobbies of the major shops (Ogilvy, BBDO, Young & Rubicam), plus a few fast-rising boutiques, and handed my résumé off to the receptionists along with the confident and personable smile of a creative God.

I booked two interviews the old-fashioned way. The first man proposed meeting me for a drink because he "had to meet the guy insane enough to hand out his CV in person." Whatever that meant. And, of course, the smartass no-showed.

The other creative director who slotted me in forgot about our meeting, and from the alarming grimace twisting across her face when I sat down, she found my plucky presence unwelcome, if not hostile.

And as I walked her through the multilayered context woven through my top headlines—like my mocked-up ad for a street-legal Humvee: *At Last, Men Can Buy Size*—she started crying.

Christ, is my book that bad?

"I'm sorry, Mark," she said.

"Jason."

"Whatever. I just got fired. We all did."

She buried her head in her hands and blew up sobbing. I got up slowly and backed away, disappointed but also thrilled the cause of her life's ruin had zip to do with my portfolio.

Back outside in single-digit temperatures, I began the grim trudge north, back to my pied-à-terre, opting out of a cozy ride on the subway because I needed a brisk walk to cool off the demons cackling in my head.

Somewhere along the way, around 56th Street, I stopped walking and started to chuckle. The chuckle turned into a deep, hearty laugh, escalating into a wounded howl, likely reminding anyone to pass by of John Hurt's portrayal of *The Elephant Man*.

I got back to walking and thought about the opening credits of *The Mary Tyler Moore Show*. Young and wholesome, Mary moved to Minneapolis with an earnest dream. And when her dream became a reality, Mary, so overloaded with joy, broke down in the middle of the city during rush hour and hurled her tacky blue knit beret high into the air. On the other hand, I ducked into a seedy liquor store and bought a fifth of scotch.

For the next three weeks, I remained barricaded in my flophouse room, fleshing out a plan B on a legal pad and drinking heroic amounts of scotch out of a waxy plastic cup from a deli.

Then through a fluke encounter, I connected with a friend from college who happened to be attending Columbia's prestigious J-School. He liked the idea of splitting his rent. And I liked the idea of not waking up to being murdered or, worse, continuing to shower in my motel's community bathroom. So, I moved in and took over the foldout couch in his studio apartment, which was the size of a modest toolshed.

I made peace with advertising's swift rejection of my work and didn't bother wiping the stench off my book before jamming another ridiculous dream down the building's trash chute.

Oddly, as I did the backstroke each day through a full fifth of scotch, my confidence outgrew all sense of reason, which led me to pursue a more sensible line of work—writing topical monologue jokes for David Letterman or Conan O'Brien and, in the worst case, Jon Stewart.

I started picking up the paper each morning at a corner store, along with a six-pack, and spent the day stringing four to five jokes together intended for an unnamed late-night television host to recite and keep middle-America in stitches.

Earlier this week, Miss America contestants took a tour of the White House. They got a nice surprise when President Clinton came out of the Oval Office to say hello. Isn't that nice, Paul? Yeah, then, as a parting gift, he handed them his pants.

One of my college professors, whom I admired and thought of as a mentor of sorts, had a connection. In his former life as a television writer, he got to know Letterman's top scribe. And I made sure to spread my professor's respectable name across every inch of my snappy cover letter, which I hand-delivered (!) to the Ed Sullivan Theater, attached to twenty pages of the least lame jokes I cobbled together over the past few weeks out of thin air.

I didn't hold my breath waiting for a response, but when an assistant from the show phoned me a week later with Dave's head writer waiting on the line, I understood, finally, the miraculous disbelief Moses tried describing to his skeptical buddies after getting off the phone with God.

"Dave tells the jokes the way he wants. Never write the way you think he talks. He hates that," he said.

"Of course. Okay," I answered.

"You're funny. This is good stuff," he said.

To me, this sounded like a job offer, but instead, I learned Dave's team was adequately staffed. Plus, a homeless mob of *Lampoon* flunkies from Harvard erected a shantytown in the alley behind his show and begged for work every morning like hobos desperate for a ladle of hot cream soup. And the call ended.

Remarkably, I didn't stroll out to Amsterdam Avenue and hop in front of an oncoming bus. I mean, at worst, the head writer of *The Late Show* liked my jokes. And with the currency of my self-worth plummeting downward like a watermelon tossed from Dave's studio roof, I squeezed the compliment like a rotten orange and mixed the resulting drop of positivity with cheap red wine and bar scotch, which helped decrease the breakneck speed of my plunge.

Over the next few weeks, through a sequence of foggy events, I found myself working as a nonpaid intern at an independent film production company way downtown in SoHo. They did something to acquire fractional points on the gross of the movie *Sling Blade*, starring Billy Bob Thornton.

In the movie, Billy Bob played a sickle-swinging, dim-witted, barn-raised psychopath who got off lurking around the backwoods of Arkansas and chewing on straw. And for reasons lost on me, his loony-bird character became hell-bent on protecting a young boy from something mysterious but decidedly worse than anyone's most appalling guess. But it was probably from all the other brain-dead hillbillies living in the forest, famous for boiling young boys into their onion and squirrel stew when they weren't making wild berry jam and toxic moonshine. A reasonable conclusion considering the movie took place in Arkansas.

And this being the '90s, overcooked character studies shot on shoestring budgets made a habit out of cleaning up every March at the Oscars. This trend elevated disturbing little movies like *Sling Blade*, at least in the mind of one scumbag producer, into something more desirable than uncut coke sitting on a sweet hooker's ass.

So, no surprise, Miramax showed up with a sack full of cash, bought the lion's share of the rights, and distributed the movie behind the total weight of their influential art-house brand and made a fortune.

Whatever the case, the production company I worked for took their fractional scraps of the box office proceeds to finance gritty street movies set in Queens, widely mocked as Tarantino rip-offs. They let me do all the grunt work during shoots. I ran errands, delivered movie equipment to sets, and played a background actor in one of the films they shot.

My epic scene took place in an insane asylum. I portrayed a man sitting alone at a table, staring at a chessboard with crazy eyes. And when the lead character walked into the scene, I slammed the chessboard to the floor and stormed off, grunting and howling like a stuck pig. In the end, nobody confused my work with Brad Pitt's introductory scene in *Thelma & Louise*. And how could they? The crummy picture never made it to postproduction.

Eventually, I worked my way into the literature department, reading screenplays submitted by writers from all over the country. I wrote coverage and passed the decent scripts over to the producers for consideration with my snarky notes. The sheer volume of printed garbage showing up each day shocked me. At least forty feature-length scripts. Each one, more ridiculous than the last. But I drew deep satisfaction from reading them and providing obsessively detailed feedback. More so, the things I learned from reading scripts all day provided the embellished confidence I needed to start writing a screenplay on my own.

In less than a month, I cranked out the first draft of an epic road picture about two college buddies who moved to New York. One character dreamed of becoming an investment banker, while the other targeted his sights on joining the cast of *Saturday Night Live*. But the city thrust them from her bowels before they found futons for their crummy apartment. So now, too embarrassed to go home as total failures, they fled to Mexico and entered a high-stakes international margarita-making contest where the winner took home $100,000. Gosh, a tidy sum like that might go a long way to help two college-aged fellas on the snide turn their lives around. Duh, ya think?

But wouldn't you know, in an "outrageous" mix-up, they find themselves on the wrong side of the event's secret sponsor, who happens to be a ruthless drug lord who wanted to win the contest for his own nefarious reasons. Naturally, one of the characters falls in love before all hell breaks loose. *The Margarita Incident*, starring Matthew McConaughey and an Ethan Hawke type, only grungier and, if possible, more solemn. Coming soon never!

I did all my writing late at night and on Saturday afternoons. And if the movie's boozy title and the half-baked plot failed to clarify, I did so while drinking myself blind.

On one of these Saturdays, lost in a beautiful fog of creative output, the phone rang and yanked me back into the dull and predictable real world.

The one where two ordinary college-aged guys aren't forced to fight a three-hundred-pound gimp (who never lost) in a win-or-die underground cage match. Annoyed, I answered the phone, regretting my choice instantly.

"So, Madison Avenue capped your knees already?" my dad said.

"I decided on a different direction. Working on a screenplay, now," I answered.

I could hear his eyes roll. "Screenwriters aren't writers; they're more like paid whores," my dad said. The sluggish pace of his voice made it clear he'd jumped off the wagon, mouth first, into a pool of bourbon.

"Lucky them. I'm still giving mine away for free."

Like father like son. Both alone, drunk, and feisty. But instead of defending my turf by demolishing his, I refused to engage. And in doing so, I discovered how life feels when time stops. After an agonizing spell of black silence, I told him a friend of mine from home got sent to town on business, and I planned a wild night for us in the city.

"Enjoy the fun. Because friendships don't last. Your friends will disappear. They always do," he said.

"Are you working at Hallmark, Dad?" I asked.

He chuckled. And we fell back into our normal silent standoff, scored by the eerie hum of our tormented relationship and the sounds we made, swallowing mouthfuls of whatever sat in front of us. In my case, a Beefeater gin mixed with 7 Up.

"Goddammit, Dad, you're killing me," I said.

He got out two or three words I didn't catch before I slammed down the phone.

A new girl joined our growing team of interns at the production company. She came to New York via Georgia as a recent graduate from a southern school. A charming and effervescent sorority girl who failed in covering that part of herself up by wearing Doc Marten boots and a leather jacket, both black.

We became friends right off the bat. She and I hit different bars together after work in and around SoHo. I enjoyed her company, as the city started becoming lonely and impossible, despite the fast development of my script.

One evening after going to a bar, I picked up a few bottles of wine, and we decided to polish them off at her place. She lived in a fabulous apartment, at least for an unpaid intern, located on the Upper East Side.

We both loved to drink and listen to ourselves talk. And many nights, we rambled on well past two in the morning. While I uncorked the wine and filled our glasses with a heavy pour, she told me (half embarrassed) her grandfather wrote a few famous songs in the '40s, and the royalties set her family up for life.

"Trust me, I couldn't pay for this," she said.

After a few weeks of this, she made plans to fly home to Atlanta for the weekend and wanted to hit the bars before leaving. As we threw back drinks at the first bar, two well-dressed men started chatting her up. Their attention sparked her up, and she flirted back in a way I think she thought would bother me. But it didn't, which annoyed her.

I liked her, but my immediate intentions focused on getting the next drink. And foolishly for Lucia, I sealed off the part of my heart capable of giving and receiving the type of affection expected in a normal relationship, like boarding up a summer home at season's end.

We decided to go to her apartment and drink through the night. When we got inside, I wished right away we had parted ways at the bar. On the walk over, I became agitated, suddenly consumed with getting back to my studio apartment to uncork a bottle and hammer away on my script.

"Hey, I gotta go," I said.

"Right," she laughed.

"I need to work on my script."

This sounded so ridiculous I felt like an idiot saying it. We both knew Lucas, Spielberg, or the male prostitutes selling star maps on Melrose weren't aware of my script or my existence on earth. I didn't like being a jerk, but I turned to leave. She didn't walk me to the door or say goodbye.

On the street and energized by my heavy buzz, I considered crossing the park on foot. A brisk walk to clear the head. But I realized I forgot my backpack upstairs, which held a printed copy of my script with all the redlines, not to mention my keys and wallet. And since her flight to Atlanta took off in less than eight hours, I had no choice but to turn around and head back. I knocked on her door, which she opened right away, crying.

"You came back?" she said.

She smiled and approached me for an embrace, hugging me as if we hadn't seen each other in years. I owed her a hug back.

"Uh, I forgot my backpack," I said.

At this point, Nicholas Sparks hadn't written *The Notebook* (I think), but if she ever got around to reading his book or struggled through the movie years later in a theater, I doubt her memory of this moment came beaming back to romantic life.

When I got back to my apartment, the clock read 2:00 a.m. I grabbed a dirty glass out of the sink, thrilled two unopened bottles of wine stood on the counter. I uncorked the first. And as wine splashed into the cup, I listened to the electrifying sounds of the city, reminding me of the infinite opportunity bustling outside beneath me, close enough to touch, even at two in the morning.

I let out a deep breath and gazed around. Here I was, sitting in my tumbledown studio apartment, drinking thin wine from a smudged glass, and diving back into the creation of a screenplay sure to catapult me to stardom. As happy and content as I'd ever been.

Out of habit, I checked the voice mail. One message. Of course. Probably a sad drunken rant from my friend across the park. I braced myself.

"Hey, it's your brother. Call me back when you get this."

We didn't often talk. Plus, I was drunk. I called him back right away.

"Everything okay?" I asked.

"Well, kind of depends. It's Dad. He died."

THE HOLLYWOOD
SCUFFLE

Six months after my dad's funeral, I migrated west, drafting behind the million other desperadoes drawn in by the honeysuckle scent of easy money and quick fame. I touched down during the peak of a frenzied spec script boom.

My impatient and greedy flames got fanned each day in the *Hollywood Reporter* with captivating profiles featuring another starry-eyed nitwit from nowhere who sold a buddy-cop script to a top studio for a million dollars and points on the gross.

Stories like this attracted "writers" from all over the world. And we descended on Los Angeles like rabid flocks of seagulls, as if everything between Silver Lake and Santa Monica reeked of sweet beach garbage.

If my dad's death took the shine off my experience in New York, opening the door to his home in Santa Barbara made the world pitch black. The way he died, and the haunting evidence he left behind as proof his departure was planned, moved me to take immediate action.

So, I submitted my script *The Margarita Incident* to the UCLA screenwriting program, then sent them a tuition check, knowing I'd run Hollywood before the last class got dismissed.

Getting accepted into UCLA gave me a needed boost in my expired confidence and dared me to think less horribly about myself as a writer and, I guess, a person. And moving to LA delivered a substantial buzz which lasted all the way up to the welcome reception on the UCLA campus when I started meeting my peers.

At the program's meet and greet, before snagging a third house red from the roaming waiter's tray, I realized any moron with enough cash and the ability to fog a mirror secured a seat in this program. And I'm sure loopholes existed for any applicant incapable of drawing a breath.

I took a long moment to survey the reception room, crowded with hopeful idiots like me, a distressing scene, sending me into a panic. I tried foraging through the dubious sequence of events leading me to this place. But my frenzied birdbrain sat stock-still, exhausted from dragging my overweight and reckless aspirations cross-county, a load better suited for a garbage scow.

Spinning a single reality-based reason up to support why moving here differed from my deep collection of self-destructive, boneheaded decisions proved impossible. I started planning my move to the mountains (I heard good things about Telluride) to live out the rest of my years as a delusional ski bum. (While writing a contrived script about it—*Snowed Out!*)

The waiter shuffled by again, and I yanked another sour wine off his tray. And suddenly, for no material reason, my mood shot up. Maybe I snorted in a scented sniff of a California spicebush or caught a lucky and sanctified glimpse of the setting sun's deep rosy reflection radiating off a campus building's double-glazed window. I can't be sure. But an elusive spark triggered an energizing release of bullish exuberance, reminding me where in the hell I lived.

I'm in LA.

A magical city built on synthetic positivity and blind hope. The same place where a thousand agents, directors, and producers woke up this same morning between two dead hookers and still snagged a front-row cycle in Spin class, smiling no less. The show must go on.

I poured everything into my script and committed to UCLA's program to learn from the best. Regardless of the deplorable way I judged my classmates (all groundless), the writing professors teaching us came with incredible résumés.

But in less than a month, I sensed a chilling disturbance in the force flipping through the professor's profile pages. And the

freezing power grew in intensity the more I reread each instructor's long list of notable writing credits.

Let me explain. Yes, each professor wrote at least one big-time
movie, and a couple owned an admirable collection of the industry's top awards. Yet, what should've been a source of validating
inspiration instead created an effect every bit as frosty as Keyser
Söze's reveal at the end of *The Usual Suspects*.

For starters, why in the hell did these movie-writing titans com-
mute to Westwood from Burbank? Plus, they all drove banged-up
sedans as plain as pea-green flowerpots, like a fleet of unmarked
squad cars pulled off the set of a low-budget movie about worka-
day cops. What about all the millionaire screenwriters glamorized
daily in the trades? The ones zipping around the respectable parts
of LA in shiny 911s with bank sacks under the hood and stunning
models/actresses bouncing on their laps?

My overall concerns about the program escalated once we
broke off into groups to do table reads. In my group, not one of us
clicked. And why would we? Nobody came here to make friends
but, instead, to wrap our greedy mitts around the world's most
guarded pile of money and materialize the scantest degree of fame.
Two singular and merciless objectives harder to come by than a
stenciled invite from Hugh Hefner to a Playmate orgy.

So, each week we brought in printed pages, assigned roles from
the script to our classmates, and acted out the writer's scenes
for the sole purpose of learning. Sounds super helpful, right? But
our obsessive and needy quest to earn a nonmaterial amount of

Hollywood's invented approval, financial or otherwise, turned the weekly table reads into an unparalleled demonstration of a human's capacity to maximize the elastic reaches of passive-aggressive behavior.

What can a writer learn about his beloved script when the people trusted to read its lines, in character, are the same people hoping the author gets splattered by a Humvee screaming through a red light at Wilshire and Fairfax?

All the actionable and quick-firing stage directions written with hypereconomic prose to keep the action moving (*Ted walks in; Jane pulls out a knife.*) were vocalized to sound like a brain-damaged repairman talking to his favorite wrench.

Likewise, I played dirty too. I specialized in forgetting my turn to read, which of course, in the unlikely event a scene's momentum generated dramatic heat, the words, "Um, what's my line?" made quick work of destroying the moment faster than finding a bulge under a blind date's dress.

But I found reading a lead character's most pivotal statement as a floaty and improbable question packed the most punch.

"I'm going to…destroy, every…last one…of you…bastards?"

We also treated each other's minor typos with exaggerated, self-righteous hysteria. An unnecessary comma generated more fevered anger than a towering portrait of the devil's privates spray-painted on the side of a small-town church. Afterward, we managed to sit through open critiques—more misleading than brutal—somehow without killing each other.

For example, a "helpful" suggestion from the group might sound like this:

"I know Don is your hero. And the audience must love him. But he needs some flaws, you know, to make him relatable. So, like, make him a racist or something, right?"

The one thing I left the program with was a soothing, narcissistic level of self-baked superiority. I thought of my classmates and the teachers slumming in the 818 as hacks. Everybody wanted to be the next Tarantino but was too busy extracting the last spongy specs of bone marrow out of the *Die Hard* trope. Except for one guy, a quiet drifter, whose comedy script *Buttons Down* escalated *Bio-Dome* into high art.

When the program ended, I rejoiced. And getting an up-close view of the competition gave me all the self-assurance I needed to pop out of bed every morning to shave and keep writing.

During this time, I applied scientific thought into perfecting my writer's routine—the same one I started toying with in high school. Over time, leveraging trial and error, I continued making tweaks and adjustments to amplify my daily writing's quality and output.

In short, I drank whatever amount of alcohol kept the pages spinning out of the printer. And once, in the interest of scientific discovery, when my friends and I came home from a three-day golf marathon in Rosarito Beach, I smuggled back enough Mexican speed to keep a long-haul trucker's eyelids peeled back for a year.

Unfortunately, velocity beans didn't work for me. I mean, sure, pharmaceutical-grade speed worked. But I found writing to be complicated while scrubbing the ceiling with a toothbrush and screaming at the birds (real or imagined) cackling outside my window. I mean, writing is hard enough, no?

The routine I started slipping on with the ease of a driving loafer began with two stout cocktails each evening, always anchored with a mid-range scotch. Next, I uncorked and nursed a magnum of cheap table wine until my cloudy thoughts formed into words.

What's more, I injected gobs of nicotine into my bloodstream. I smoked the occasional pack of cigarettes. But for the most part, I stuck to stuffing my cheeks and lips with smokeless tobacco, like a squirrel packing up campsite trash before a fast-approaching arctic freeze.

I practiced this routine Monday through Friday, every night until I stopped writing or blacked out. And my system worked. Because in less time than it takes a cab to cross town in the rain, *The Margarita Incident* caught the eye of a producer, and he scooped up the rights to produce a feature film on an eighteen-month option.

Moreover, I negotiated an associate producer role to help bring my baby to the screen and, of course, lobby to play one of the lead roles. Welcome to Los Angeles, babe.

For the next few weeks, I flew around Los Angeles weightless and pleasantly stunned one of my stupid dreams came true. But I started spending less time writing and more time with my nose buried in the paper's real estate section. Where should I live when they back up the money truck? Malibu? Too far from the action.

Beverly Hills? Overrated. Hancock Park? Meh. Renting a cozy bungalow behind the Chateau Marmont made the most sense.

I daydreamed about me writing by the pool all day after taking shots with DiCaprio and getting wrestled to the ground by Uma Thurman the night before. I never moved through days this alive, this complete, and so excited. My life's narrative swiveled toward becoming one of the most beautiful and meaningful Hollywood clichés ever imagined.

But while sorting out the pesky details of my fabulous life, I couldn't help noticing the producer who bought the rights to my script stopped returning my calls. And no matter how many times I checked the mailbox per day, the check for the option never came.

All things considered, I still called Los Angeles home. La-La Land. The Big Orange. The only city on earth where a chance encounter at the gas pump might shoot your fortunes through the moon.

So instead of hitting the panic button, I dialed up the intensity of my writer's routine (meaning more scotch and wine) and dove into fleshing out my follow-up script: *Buttons Down 2: Zippy Kai Yay, Motherfucker!*

THE GOLDEN
GRATE

L os Angeles flaunts plenty to love. The dreamy vibe. The perfect weather. And how the coagulation of chain restaurants and national stores personifying the 3rd Street Promenade in Santa Monica didn't look like a suburban stain, another greedy money shot left behind by a predatory builder when he finished his business and pulled out.

But once the traditional studios, independent producers, and the homeless man who used my trash can as a toilet indicated zero interest in my scripts, my attitude toward Los Angeles, like the ground beneath her, started to crack.

My drinking program reduced me down to a soaked rag, only weaker. Every day played out the same. I drove by the gym without stopping until I pulled into the liquor store, loaded up, and sped home, where I inspected the mailbox for a million-dollar check stapled to a three-picture deal from DreamWorks or Paramount. The check never came.

After tossing my unopened mail in the trash, I started drinking until the courage came, enabling me to eyeball the festering stack of crap on my desk I didn't remember writing from the night before. Now, with my brain as clear as mud, I opened my laptop and started banging out more crap to add to the stack. At some point, I passed out. Then started all over in the morning, like *Groundhog Day* in hell.

As Mr. Rogers famously said of a child's life, "Quick to ripe, long to rot." 'Twas a dark time, indeed.

Often, I found myself confusing Los Angeles for the actor Nicolas Cage, because both are fascinating enough to draw you in and keep you engaged and entertained, if not mesmerized. But on a whim, both can bite your ear off and stab you through the heart with a screwdriver, leaving you to bleed out behind a dumpster and more confused about the folly of life than Fleetwood Mac after Jamiroquai edged them out for a Grammy.

And yet, not everything I viewed appeared pitch black. As a matter of fact, something resembling light, a subtle glow, started glistening out of the long-stagnant relationship Lucia and I recently rekindled. This sentimental and lovey-dovey development, paired with my own inextinguishable dream of hitting Hollywood pay dirt, made up the only two things keeping me from starting random water balloon fights at Salazar Park or doing Tai Chi blindfolded in the middle of the 405 after midnight. And since she lived up the road in San Francisco, I maintained a good reason to bust the hell out of LA every few weeks to drive up and hang out.

I fell madly in love with San Francisco. Of course, the city and its surroundings make that an easy proposition. But I came to think the city dwellers played a bigger part in making the Bay Area a transcendent kind of never-never land.

Everyone I met moved to San Francisco from far away and brought, along with their Patagonia pullovers and Salomon trail boots, meaningful intentions attached to detailed lists of sensible steps on how to make them happen. Change the world. Save the world. Or smoke a few bowls and write a song about the people trying (and failing).

To me, the vibe in Northern California personified the state's original personality. Or at least how I remembered the West Coast as a child. In San Francisco, people played outdoors, ate healthy foods, and looked forward to waking up tomorrow. And if anyone needed additional inspiration, they dropped into Peet's for a triple shot of espresso, which packed a bigger punch than ten lines of blow.

When I compared people's motivating drivers to my own (instant fame, easy riches, and courtside seats to the Lakers), I struggled believing my future held more promise than a clogged toilet at Candlestick Park.

Whenever I drove up to San Francisco, I arrived at 5:00 p.m. sharp to start happy-hour drinking before putting down my bag. Lucia's vibrant and outgoing circle of friends always reserved a massive table at an impossibly unique restaurant. But by the time we arrived at 9:00 p.m. to eat, my eyeballs floated in wine, and I never touched a fork.

After dinner, the bars we hit were these perfect, dark little places, likely less cool than I imagined them. Regardless, we closed them down and flocked to an apartment in the Marina or Pacific Heights and kept drinking and dancing well into the morning.

More than once, coffee tables became makeshift stages for clogging demonstrations performed by Lucia and one of her roommates. And in my blissful stupor, at this hour, their impromptu dance numbers made Michael Flatley look like the whitest dad on earth doing the running man at an Irish wedding after draining the open bar.

Lucia and I sort of dated now. A status we revoked toward the end of college, over three years back. No question, we loved each other. But the substantial amount of time and distance between the freewheeling days in college and the present blew out most of the flames of our initial fire. We often spoke about meeting too soon. This existential conversation touched on destiny and fate and the folly of governing either with laws, logic, or a Magic 8-Ball. Afterward, we ate lunch at a chic bistro, of course.

More and more, while loading up my emotional belongings before heading home, I chewed on how heavy the unpacking and packing of them weighed on my heart. Not an issue if I kept feelings stored in a shaving kit. This intermittent cohesiveness wreaked havoc on her too. At least, I chose to believe so.

Of course, unlike me, she surrounded herself with a community of loving friends who never let her come down with the suicidal Sunday blues. And though I got along fine with them, an unspoken understanding implied they each knew a better version of me. In fact, one that was ten thousand times better. In one call, they'd have him banging down Lucia's door, roses in hand, before the morning fog burned off the second I mucked her charmed life up.

They reminded me about this fact on every visit. Usually, as I packed up for the lonely drive back to Los Angeles, her room-mates made a telegraphic fuss getting themselves (and Lucia) primped up for a bottomless flute brunch with some clean-cut yanks "embarrassed" about graduating from Princeton. Although, anytime I partied with them, they never shut up about their "little college in New Jersey."

One Sunday, this self-destructive way of saying goodbye nearly killed me. The night before, we did the usual. Early drinks followed by a Michelin-rated dinner I didn't touch, all topped off by tabletop dancing and vodka gulping until four in the morning.

The resulting hangover's total sum of shame and pain figured too complex to calculate using the trusted formulas of action-reaction math. Too many variables, weighted and unknown, for my simple human brain to categorize and solve for this level of dread. Perhaps figuring out a hangover's riddle wasn't meant to be. As if staring at the precise and unfeeling answer at the bottom of a whiteboard would make my head explode. If a lesson existed, I could only grasp fractional meaning if considered through the more ambiguous narratives rooted in Greek mythology.

For example, suppose my arms grew tired from excessive flapping, and my body glowed with third-degree burns and melted beeswax. If so, I might better understand Icarus's thoughts about flying toward the sun. Conclusions he mustered up sinking to the bottom of the ocean at the speed of a steel shaft weighing ten tons. But of course, I'm pretty sure he died before he learned his lesson, if he learned anything at all.

At any rate, in my current condition, if one of my day's top goals included not dying in a horrible, fiery crash, I had a better chance of achieving this by jumping the Snake River in a Winnebago.

Thinking about the drive caused me to break out in an icy sweat, stinging my skin. Plus, I preferred not to leave Lucia. Again. And specifically, a few minutes before she and her roommates started splashing around in a pool of champagne with a pack of Princeton blowhards.

I longed to share the kind of overwhelming and constant love flushing through every cell in our bodies, cleansing out the toxic doubt, replenishing the circuitry with a giddy, cure-all elixir.

These goodbyes rotted critical chunks of my heart, and each time one happened, I wondered if this farewell embrace would be our last. On the first few miles of every drive home, I cried like a baby while trying hard to imagine any scenario where our relationship didn't implode.

Thankfully, during Jimmy Carter's presidency, I had recognized my God-given talent: an innate ability to smother out my emotions. And ever since then, I nurtured and strengthened my unique set of skills with the same dogged pluck an Olympic-bound ice skater poured into landing a triple Lutz.

This enabled me to muffle out the sappy pain and related imagery (celebrating my fiftieth birthday alone at Wendy's, shopping at Walmart in pajamas, discussing movies with my best friend Nick, an argyle sock puppet) before Sunnyvale, where I usually veered off the 101 to fill up with gas and purchase all the Gatorades my two hands could hold.

But this time, I let my emotions live and zoomed through Sunnyvale, blubbering, driving through visions of Nick (the argyle sock) and me passed out on a recliner in front of the tube. Making matters worse, the world's meanest little beast of a hangover sat coiled behind me, kicking the back of my seat and screaming like a red paper wasp stung his inexplicably exposed pecker.

After chewing up some more road, I managed to settle down, but my brain flatlined, and I couldn't keep my eyes open any longer, so I pulled off the 101 in San Luis Obispo. With nothing guiding me but a primal need, I rolled into a motel with a log cabin motif and a glowing red neon sign alerting all comers about their available rooms.

I dragged myself into the office and was greeted by a frumpy but sneaky beautiful woman with wet gray hair combed back atop an angelic face, recently scrubbed, I presumed, with organic lavender soap. She appeared to be in her sixties and glowed with a peaceful aura, like someone unaware of the world's most awful things tormenting the rest of us. Nasty things like disease, terrorism, and the commercial success of bands like Chumbawamba.

Looking at her, I gathered she pulled more life out of planting herbs in the clay pots behind her barn than a thousand Charlie Sheens could by sailing around the world on a mega-yacht packed with strippers and an unlimited supply of Colombia's best coke. But who am I to say? It's just as likely she spent all day sucking sweet green smoke from a tower bong taller than her tits standing on a shoebox.

I entered the room. And my mood lifted before the click of the closing door, buoyed by heavy air carrying nosy scents of natural soaps and artisan candles. The clean bed boasted pillows perfectly placed and conveyed a worn-in softness unable to trigger a stream of grim thoughts about how the mattress got pounded into such an inviting shape. Instead, all I thought about was the relief waiting for me on the other side of history's most incredible roadside nap.

I woke up in the dark. I slipped out of bed, took a hot shower, and shaved my face. Refreshed, I dressed and walked outside, up to and along the main street, passing artsy shops closed for the night and various restaurants until I found a quintessential-looking small-town steakhouse with soft lighting and rugged wooden walls stained dark. Perfect.

I took a seat at the bar, and the pleasant and ruddy bartender said hello like she relished greeting me. We chatted about the local wines. And based on the inadequate, unfounded drivel spewing out of my mouth about wine and wine making, she devised the appropriate recommendation. I thought telling her I came prepared to guzzle wine from a spit bucket did little to enhance the quality of our amiable conversation.

She grabbed a clean-limbed green bottle off a shelf, poured a generous amount into a mason jar, and placed the drink in front of me. I took a mouthy gulp. Seconds later, the wine's heat, as quick as a rifle shot, immobilized the unrestrained torment galloping through my head. All the jagged depression and anxiety vanished without a trace. Only a space-like hum of well-being remained, and I melted into my chair. The bartender kept the generous pours coming. I ate one of the better steaks ever served. And chased down one more monster glass of wine, flooding the rest of my angst into tomorrow.

On the way back to my room, I struggled. Not because I became too drunk and found walking straight impossible. But being so energized and happy, I feared the end of this sweet buzz. I recalled having two bottles of wine in my car and hustled straight to the motel parking lot at a brisk clip.

I got to my car and stood frozen, stuck in a conscious state of contemplative indecision, an enigmatic sensation I experienced more often than brushing my teeth.

For reasons still unclear, I decided to end the night. I went back to my room, got myself into bed, and flipped through the TV's channels to keep myself distracted. Restless and hot, I jumped up and opened the window, letting the nippy Central Coast nighttime air cool the room. I curled back up in bed and turned out the lights, smiling, still bemused with relief for not corking open the first of those two bottles. When I nodded off, I slept like a hibernating bear.

The next day, I woke up with a slight hangover, the good kind of hangover, capable of clearing my head, if not invigorating for the whole rest of me. Before leaving town, I found a no-frills diner and ordered a pot of coffee with a spinach-and-Monterrey-Jack-cheese omelet. San Luis Obispo is halfway between Los Angeles and San Francisco. Driving toward the 101, the idea occurred to me, not a single reason or obstacle on earth kept me from heading north instead of south. I pulled over and thought about this freedom of choice with a heavy heart for many reasons. Both sound and stupid.

I sat idling at a literal crossroads. And I soon realized neither direction led to anything heartfelt and meaningful. I missed the motel and considered making a U-turn, getting another room, and vowing to never leave. I could plant my wandering roots here, in the nourishing soil underneath this town, and not one single person on earth could stop me. Or care enough to try.

What if I got a job at the local paper selling ads? Soon, I would work my way into having my own insightful and observational weekly column (*Keep Looking!*), in which I poked fun of the big-city tourists, all burnouts who appeared rangier and more hopeless than me before finally finding my home.

My new friends might talk about interesting books and yoga, or how great being a vegetarian is without sounding like all the horrible, self-aggrandizing dirtbag posers living up the road and sucking the soul out of San Francisco. Or perhaps fall in with a group of like-minded folks not hell-bent on drinking.

If I stayed here, I would enroll in graduate school, pick up a master's in English lit, and teach a popular creative writing class at the local high school, like a less insane version of Robin Williams in *Dead Poets Society*.

After class, I would take my students' papers home, which I inspired them to write, reading them with a glass of wine. Only one glass. And after writing each student a personal and detailed note complimenting their work, my dog, a white golden retriever named, of course, Nick, and I would stroll through town. This all sounded so perfect and necessary and right.

I shifted the car into drive, continuing west down the main street toward the 101. And without another thought, manic or otherwise, I flipped my blinker downward, indicating to the indifferent motorists behind me, my life was heading south, down toward Los Angeles, driving straight back to hell. I couldn't do this anymore.

CAT AND SOUSE

I n 2000, recognizing the sentimental gravity keeping our souls grounded on the same planet continued strengthening since the day we met, I proposed to Lucia, and we got married. She enrolled in graduate school at USC, and we settled in Los Angeles as loving, if not bewildered, newlyweds.

We moved into a one-bedroom walk-up apartment located in the flats of Beverly Hills. A quiet, modest neighborhood allowing for a pseudopedestrian lifestyle, which, along with meaningful friendships and sympathetic meter maids, is unusual to find in LA.

On most nights, I strolled to Whole Foods to pick up fixings for dinner, including inappropriate amounts of wine. Other times, we meandered up and down South Beverly (between Wilshire and

Gregory), ducking into sushi or pizza joints for a quick bite before going to one of LA's dearly missed newsstands, where we flipped through magazines until one of our favorite shows started: *The Sopranos*, *The West Wing*, or *Who Wants to Be a Millionaire*.

Our first Christmas tree shared the size and charisma of an everyday table plant. Nevertheless, like giddy kids playing grown-up, we decorated the "tree" with tiny ornaments, using enough twinkling white lights to impress Clark Griswold.

But the bubbly effects of our newlywed buzz turned flat before the houseplant began to wilt. Over the holidays, all at once, Los Angeles turned evil. The civic abnormalities I conditioned myself to tolerate (the smog, the road rage, Cameron Crowe winning an Oscar for *Almost Famous*) made me wish Skynet from *T2* existed and was in the process of counting down.

Plus, while sharing a home with Lucia, drinking two bottles of wine every night proved to be tricky business without tripping the alarm bells, introducing me to new, shameful behaviors. For example, buying tiny, four-ounce screw-top bottles of sour wine by the handful to slug down on my walk back home from Whole Foods. Or duck into our favorite cafe, alone, for a couple of fast tequila shots chased down by an aggressive Malbec.

As a brain-damaged engineer might deduce, these practical solutions don't scale, and I resented staying ahead of the increasing complexity required to disguise the heroic amounts of wine I drank each night, beginning the moment I moved to New York.

The sanctity of marriage (for better or worse?) failed to stomp out childish games of cat and mouse. And all the necessary planning and scheming added an unexpected load on top of a marital foundation still under construction and incapable of handling additional stress.

So I caulked over the cracks drinking created with a toxic paste, a homemade mix of simmering bitterness and heightened resentment. I hated doing this. But I hated covering up wine stains, riddled with shame, lest I get browbeaten like a vagrant trespasser if I didn't.

All my lying friends glorifying the honeymoon phase must've been abusing their prescribed medications by the bucket to lessen the pain of their souls getting cracked in half.

To be fair, I sympathized with Lucia and considered that back when she fantasized about marriage, as a doe-eyed little princess, more than likely she imagined something a tad different too.

But the eight-hundred-pound gorilla jerking off in the room was my irrefutable sense of self. I mean, here I was, married to the one girl God wired together crazy enough to stick around for the next episode. The only person I dared risking a glimpse at my carved-up heart and untethered brain. The miraculous fact she stuck around to reciprocate these affections served to confirm celestial involvement.

We deemed our connection as spiritual, not luck. Immersing ourselves in deep and loopy bewildering talks on hikes up Runyon Canyon or on airy drives to Joshua Tree, soliloquizing the designed event of our souls smashing into each other like two runaway freight trains.

For the sacredness of our young, beguiling marriage, I vowed to become a better man. And a less conspicuous drinker. So with that, after counting down the seconds to her graduation, we high-tailed it east, worn down but excited about a fresh start back in Texas.

Leaving California revealed the best of us remained intact. Mutually thrilled to be driving a U-Haul, hurtling toward Texas like a meteor to live near friends and family, surrounded by gettable homes starting at $100 per foot.

Despite voyaging through lower America's scorching desert heat, we found ourselves laughing a lot, like old times. And most assuring, we passed two unannounced compatibility tests, like when the AC conked out in Death Valley. And after a sweaty slog of white-knuckle driving, we didn't spiral into a hysterical meltdown learning the only restaurant near our motel still open was a Cracker Barrel.

We landed in San Antonio, my wife's hometown. I stood up my writing dream behind a barn and shot it dead and found a tolerable place to work in IT, selling technology I didn't understand. And she signed on with an ecumenical center as a unlicensed therapist to start chipping away at the thousands of supervised hours needed before anybody struck out on their own.

Naturally, we bought the perfect starter house we couldn't afford. After which, we started reconnecting with Lucia's infinite list of friends, keeping our social calendar booked out for months in advance.

Right away, I identified a curious level of civic pride San Antonians displayed for River City's rich heritage and culture.

More interesting to me, the cadence and intensity put forward celebrating their town never stopped, primarily by getting together to consume a staggering amount of alcohol at weddings, deb parties, or mowing the lawn. In San Antonio, innocent weeknight dinner parties went well past two in the morning. And if a white-wine brunch didn't steamroll the bulk of Sunday, the remainder of the day got wiped out by a shaky round of rum-soaked golf. To be clear, baby showers without open bars went unattended, skipped by the unborn child's parents. At long last, I was home.

San Antonio is more beautiful than visitors expect. The northern part of the city pushes up against the Hill Country, while the city limit's southern edges open to the sprawling coastal plains bleeding into the Gulf. To be fair, nobody without visual impairments mixed my new hometown up with the likes of Laguna Beach or Santa Barbara. But stumbling into a city proud of their persistent affability and insatiable thirst led me to forget my home state of California existed in the first place.

Best of all, 100 percent of the people I met exemplified my tendency to drink like a hobo with an iron liver and wooden leg. I often found myself mingling with charming merrymakers a billion times more hammered and sloppier than me. An unfamiliar, profound experience, flooding my heart with joyful verse and song.

This newfound freedom improved the quality of life. No more boozy games of cat and mouse. Never again would I park down the street to finish off a bottle of red wine uncorked at the grocery store. Instead, all I had to do was buy a pink guayabera, maintain the savvy posture of Bobo the Clown, and periodically scream *"La Viva!"* whenever the Eye of Sauron shifted its disapproving glare to my backside.

These people lived their lives with a refreshing lack of cockeyed remorse, unfamiliar or unconcerned with the consequential heat of tomorrow's rising sun. To think I lived my entire life like an aimless fool, subjecting myself to the restorative assurances of runaway self-loathing mixed in acidic stews of regret. So now, inspired by watching respectable and accomplished men think nothing after a hurly-burly night of boozing other than the arrival of an unshakable sense of festive joy promising to carry them through another ho-hum day, I stepped down hard on the gas pedal.

During this golden era, I grew closer with my in-laws. We loved each other's company and enjoyed dinners together no less than twice a week. One time, our animated discussion stopped and toggled over a renowned shrink they considered hiring. At the time, somebody close to them got lost at sea. Now helpless and sailing through psychogenic waters that made *The Perfect Storm's* climax play out like the opening credit sequence in *Captain Ron.*

This therapist earned his stripes after bailing the equivalent of Lake Huron out of a wealthy family's battered boat. And now, this family pimped him like their best earner. They shared lurid details of his prowess with everyone (friends, strangers, blank-faced, non-English-speaking waiters), detailing how this mysterious miracle worker from Memphis stopped their gravy boat from sinking through the earth's core.

On top of reading *The Prince of Tides* twice, I married an up-and-coming superstar therapist. As a result, I imparted a heartfelt sentiment for the healing powers of therapy and admired the selfless people practicing the craft. So if I ever needed help, I always thought psychotherapy warranted my consideration.

Besieged by the snake charmer's praise, a twisted leeriness diverted my agreeable opinion concerning his qualifications and competency for straightening out crooked minds. I mean, people called him Big Cat. Why? Because Big Cat is the name printed on his business card. And not Dr. Big Cat. Just Big Cat.

Hearing this without an expected punchline, I pondered speeding home to crank out a script to FedEx John Goodman's agent at CAA.

Big Cat Therapy: Diagnosis: Adorable!

Big Cat Therapy: The Power of Meow!

Big Cat Therapy: This Pussy Saves Lives!

Only a few days later, my always reasonable and clear-thinking in-laws hired Big Cat for an entire week. They paid up front for an all-inclusive rate. Meaning once he showed up scratching on their front door, anyone craving a quick shot of feline mysticism could ring his bell 24/7.

Lucia surprised me by scheduling a play date with Big Cat, informing me with a casual disregard reserved for discussing the weather or dinner plans. *Great idea*, I thought. And with our first anniversary approaching, tossing some of our bouncier balls of yarn his way for feedback illustrated my commitment to self-improvement. So, I penciled down a long list of good-natured grievances ripe for discussion. If nothing else, spending an hour with a psychotherapist named Big Cat would give us plenty to laugh about on the drive home, if not for the rest of our loving lives.

Lucia set our meeting with Big Cat for Sunday afternoon. As usual, the night before, we went to a debauched shindig. In this case, a black-tie wedding. And, not surprisingly, I got ripped. Having no clue how the night ended, I woke up on the couch wearing my tuxedo as pajamas, confused why the act of breathing hurt.

By applying the mental acquisitiveness of Sherlock Holmes, I deduced a failed attempt to escape from my tie occurred at some point during the night. But instead of breaking free, I cinched the silk fabric up in a violent fit, tightening the ribbon around my throat, like polyester twine squeezing a hay bale. Upon further inspection, a red stain the size of an elephant's foot soiled the front of my white shirt, leading me to suspect a petty cat burglar climbed through a window and shot me at close range with a hot snub-nose .38. So, I decided against requesting to reschedule our appointment for Monday in the year 2030.

Lucia and I didn't speak on our way to visit Big Cat. The silent tension inside the car sucked up the breathable air.

"So, what should we do if Big Cat gets distracted by a bird in the window or starts licking his balls?" I asked, hoping to lighten the mood.

Crickets.

Her simmering aggravation coupled with my newly acquired

prickly defensiveness, I figured, might turn this routine newlywed checkup into something comparable to a dry rectal exam administered by Freddy Krueger, at least for me.

But the second Big Cat pranced in, out of his travel cage and unharnessed, my scattered nerves came to rest. Mainly because ol' Big Cat dressed like a folksy old cowboy as if his next stop took him to an open audition for a reboot of *Hee Haw*. His hayseed appearance alone exiled his presumed credibility to quack town, creating for me the pleasant effect of mainlining Valium from a garden hose.

Wrangler jeans, a starched denim shirt, and a watchband adorned with more turquoise and brushed silver than a belt buckle made in Reno. I'm no Carl Jung, but how far down the psychological rabbit hole can a frazzled couple go when the "man" leading them models his wardrobe after Grandpa Jones? I let out a deep breath and leaned way back in my chair, grinning like a Cheshire cat.

Big Cat looked us over and smiled, saying nothing. I admit, he looked and sounded the part of the nicest man on the planet. His uncomplicated presence generated a soothing lull. And I sensed he came hardwired with the innate attributes found in people boiling over with the best intentions. Overtaken by a sudden urge to crack my past wide open, starting from day one, I remembered thinking every troubled human on earth should run out and rent themselves a cat—a big one.

"Okay, so what are we discussing today?" he asked.

Then, like fingernails scraping across a blackboard, I snapped out of my breezy frame of mind, half expecting to see Sam Quint from *Jaws* staring down at us from behind.

Y'all know me. Know how I make a livin'. I'll catch this bird for you, but it ain't gonna be easy.

But the follow-up words shooting out from my wife's mouth hit me like a harpoon through the chest.

"His drinking is out of control!" she cried.

I didn't absorb another word for the rest of the session, deaf with rage. Instead, in spiteful silence, I scowled at the two condescending traitors yapping back and forth, appearing to me as melodramatic caricatures starring in a silent film. They often paused to nod in solemn agreement. While at the same time, my heart's inclination to trust humans—long tethered to a killing rack and getting stretched since third grade—seized the opportunity to expire.

Big Cat leaned in close and looked at me with his catty eyes, swollen with real tears.

"Do you recognize all the pain you're causing? You have a problem with alcohol," he said.

Ambushed and betrayed, I kept my mouth shut, bewailing with disbelief, both immediate and manic. I fantasized about standing up and walking out of the room, leaving my entire life behind (my wife, the house, myself) without sensing a twitch of regret, only the intoxicating tingle associated with new beginnings.

The increasing velocity of this raw, runaway lust burning laps around my thought track took my breath away. I panicked and slammed on the brakes.

"I've thought about it," I said.

I played along, agreeing to their cruel assessments, nodding, and telling them the bullet points in my go-forward plan. *Maybe I won't drink until Thursday. And treat weekends like a cheap wedding —beer and wine only, right?*

But I was honest about one thing, at least to myself. I did think long and hard about all the pain booze caused to my friends, family, or anyone who ever sat near me on a long flight. I thought about King Alcohol all the time, obsessively. No different from the way Sam Quint thought about sharks.

On this topic, I had no peer. And anybody foolish enough to hunt this boozy bird of mine would come to learn the hard way— they're gonna need a bigger boat.

A SHIVER
RUNS
THROUGH IT

Back when I turned eleven, fifteen pounds of fat material-ized around my belly and burrowed in for the long haul. And despite meaningful attempts to burn it off, numbering in the thousands, hauling this lump of stubborn fat around like a heavy bag stuffed with wet garbage became a normal part of life, no different from carrying my wallet or keys to my car.

Along the way, periodic upticks in life made me less consumed by this sneaky accessory of appalling girth. But when I traveled, starting at the age of thirty, this supplemental blubber provoked a stampede of shame-based emotions, trampling my mood and hope, along with every dream, even the stupid ones.

The prophetic Kate Moss validated my conventional anguish on *60 Minutes* when she explained how creeping past her allotted daily intake of one vanilla wafer and half a breath mint sent her on blind, coke-fueled rages lasting months. My soul mate.

Speaking of soul mates, eight years had eclipsed since our frisky play date with Big Cat. And if you imagine watching *Who's Afraid of Virginia Woolf* on fast-forward to the theme song from *The Benny Hill Show*, I can reclaim the thousand years needed to detail my tipsy shenanigans occurring over this pickled span of disgraceful living.

During this time, my loutish behavior replaced my lustrous brown hair as the first thing people blabbed on about or held against me. So, it shocked me we received an invitation to join friends for a week of giggles and sunshine in Bigfork, Montana.

Although I enjoyed *A River Runs Through It*, I had never considered traveling to Montana. I didn't understand or care to learn about the deeper essence affiliated with catching a slimy trout.

Instead, I liked the movie because each viewing titillated my deprived imagination into thinking Montana epitomized the perfect place for healing, offering more than towering mountains, majestic rivers, and overacted period pieces revolving around Brad Pitt.

But thanks to insufferable voice-overs, Robert Redford's

mawkish picture ages like a can of nightcrawlers left on the hood of a Jeep, as bad as any movie ever made.

Dear Jesse, as the moon lingers a moment over the Bitterroots, before its descent into the invisible, my mind is filled with song!

And yet, I still drop everything and tune in anytime it's on. Of course, the rise of my hope of Montana being a mystical cleansing center for the damned correlated with the darkening of clouds hovering over my waking life unraveling in Texas. This trip put forward a rare opportunity to correct course, so I planned on using the experience to come home a better, wiser man. No longer a convivial respite with friends in my mind, but a spiritual quest, a mission.

Then again, how many chunky people improve any part of their sluggish lives on vacation? Not counting Tom Hanks in *Cast Away*, or anybody who spent their leisure time behind bars—zero. Regardless, because my life, marriage, and ability to wear the clothes in my closet depended on getting fit, turning my body around became priority number one.

So, four months before the trip, I started running like mad. I built up to twenty-five miles per week and fabricated a customized CrossFit routine (fifty push-ups and the occasional set of jump squats) I knocked out after a jog. I tracked how much food I shoveled in my mouth and many times tried to stop.

A week before the trip, bloated with irrational optimism, I went shopping for a rustic pair of outdoor pants and a few "athletic" sweaters I didn't deserve to wear. And when I couldn't pull the front button of a thirty-four-inch pair of trousers halfway around the right side of my waist, I went Kate Moss.

I needed a miracle. Or better yet, a miracle diet. And since I spent the better part of thirty years failing them all (the cabbage soup diet, the grapefruit diet, the smoke yourself thin diet), I forged ahead, creating my own.

The disruptive spark came to me from an article describing the horrifying things French farmers put ducks through before grinding them up into foie gras. Their creative process challenged me to think like a duck. Inspiration struck! What if, rather than ramming a metal pipe down my throat and pumping a hundred pounds of grain down it until my liver burst, I used high-grade psyllium fiber and oxidized magnesium instead?

The science suggested my innovative discovery would trigger a record-breaking, cure-all bowel movement, the kind of heroic dump I dreamt about taking since bearing witness to the prodigious mound produced by the dying brachiosaurus in *Jurassic Park*.

But after my vanity project failed, I waddled onto the plane, an early morning flight, and ordered the first of five Bloody Marys.

On our first night in town, we went to a steakhouse. I asked the waiter, who quickly proved to be too slow with the wine, if he wouldn't mind wearing roller skates. Between the moment when the food server declined to the morning of the trip's last day, I don't remember a thing.

I woke up in an empty house, suffocating on the usual mix of fear and shame as I dragged myself down the stairs. The only noise came from the television. And the shrill voices from the anchors on Fox News made the grim scene more haunting and unbearable.

My brain and body failed to connect. Each step down the stairs was like playing the later stages of the game Jenga. The hazy recollection of a planned group hike, the last nature walk of the trip, gave my damaged motor skills a guilty jolt. With everyone frolicking outside, skipping through knee-high grass like neutered actors shooting a commercial for bran cereal, I sat stuck inside, violently hungover, lurching like a blob, and forever alone.

I noticed lingering proof of a hearty, communal breakfast. But no note from my wife taped to a vase of fresh-cut wildflowers. *I hope you slept well, darling. I have never loved you more than I do at this very moment!*

At least they left a clean pan on the stove, perfect for frying my brittle reasons to live down into a sour reduction sauce to smear all over a mirror.

I shuffled to the living room and crashed on the couch. In most cases, I welcomed solitude. Case in point: my biggest problem with *Cast Away* had nothing to do with Helen Hunt's spot-on portrayal of an unlovable shrill or my inability to believe a sensible man like Tom Hanks would risk his life to get her back. No, the film lost credibility sticking to the preposterous idea anyone would ever want to leave the island in the first place. Even for Kate Moss.

But now, here at rock bottom, I winced, desperate to talk with a friend. Or anyone knowledgeable about escaping boozy houses of horror. I had nobody and sat in anxious silence, too petrified to leave this haunted island on my own.

"To hell with this," I said.

I hopped up off the couch, went outside to the deck, and pulled a bottle of ice-cold white wine out of a Yeti cooler, which looked sexy enough to attack with an open-mouthed kiss. Seconds after popping off the cork, I drained a full glass. Then, in an expected and welcome response, my trusted confidant launched me into the inexplicable sensation of floating through deep space. So overcome with loving nothingness, my eyes flooded over with tears.

Five hours passed, and the only thing stopping me from drinking everything in the house and on into forever was the maddening return of my healthy friends from their uppity hike and getting reminded, with disdain, our flight home took off in less than two hours.

The day after we got home, unsure if my life hit rock bottom, I decided to weigh myself. After all, the dehydrating effects of air travel coupled with the staggering amount of alcohol I consumed over the last five days formulated a scientifically reasonable hypothesis of weighing less now than I did in third grade. A dramatic loss of weight (by any means) might spark my healthy comeback.

I pulled out the scale, getting on and off ten separate times, coming more unraveled each time the same alarming digital numbers, right down to the last unsettling ounce, projected my astonishing weight. Two hundred and thirteen pounds. An all-time high, by over twenty disgusting pounds.

By the age of thirty-five, countless men of significance made their mark. Take Steve Jobs. He came up with the iPod on his thirty-fifth birthday because the jukebox at Little Shamrock didn't play the Doors. Meanwhile, at the same age, I stood slumped in front of my bathroom mirror, nude and sapped, past my breaking point, and gagging at the repulsive caricature staring back at me. An overweight, overly sedated, and triple-hairy gorilla, more nauseous at the sight of me than I was of it.

Of course, this was as surprising as receiving junk mail. Along the way, for at least twenty years, I kept track of my alcohol-related slipups in a mental binder with detailed notes. Considering if printed, the stack of pages would reach the moon, one could argue I suffered from a slight drinking problem.

The real problem boozers call this the moment of clarity. Up to this point, I never recognized clarity as an actual thing and remained suspicious if this moment represented mine. But gazing into the reflected eyes plugged into the freakish, overweight, and hirsute gorilla before me, I reasoned it was.

As a Scot and a Presbyterian, my father believed that man, by nature, was a mess and had fallen from an original state of grace.

I thought about this overweight line from *A River Runs Through It.* So clunky and self-absorbed. Pious while being sinful. Like saying the words allowed for all kinds of mischief and sin. Then again, at this stage in my life, staring into a mirror through tears and scowling at the pale, bone-dry skin covering my haunted face, the ballsy line boosted my hope, creating, for the first time, an urge to put the bottle down.

And since my interest in getting a room at the zoo or becoming pen pals with Jane Goodall never took, I decided, at that moment, to never drink again.

Dearest Lucia, as the scorching sun lingers for an eternity over the barren wastelands crippled by the rapid expanse of nettles and mesquite, before its descent into the invisible hell beneath me, my mind is filled with song!

DON'T DRY
FOR ME,
ARGENTINA

A lcoholics Anonymous helps millions of people stay sober. Or so says the internet. But I also came across a recent survey taken by ten thousand of the program's participants, reporting only 20 percent stayed off the sauce for a span covering one to five years. A survival rate corresponding with stage 4 cancer, shark attacks, and red-eye flights on Frontier Airlines.

I supported the idea of AA and admired the hope barflies yanked out of meetings. But I resented the speed at which their dogmatic steps to recovery caused more damage to my dad's brain than the rounds of hand-to-hand combat he fought in Vietnam.

Each time he tried and failed, a curious stranger appeared, handing him a map to a secretive church basement. This basement, no doubt of wistful design, accommodated an assorted grab bag of chain-smoking drifters who shuffled around until the meeting commenced, from which they drowned in the audio pleasure of a reformed crackhead sharing his tall tales about life whipping his bare ass.

When my dad failed to quit, he got shoved back into the basement, expected to beg for another humiliating chance at redemption, like a kid who totaled the family car.

On one troubling occasion, he ran me through his written entries in *The Big Book*. And lacking the occurrence of providing each other's essential needs in a Turkish prison, this marked the most uncomfortable moment we ever shared. As a result, I spent a week researching alternate routes, trotting through the digital pastures glutted with steaming heaps of unproven horseshit.

Unexpectedly, investigating alcoholism gave my grim outlook on life an unexpected spark. The sheer volume of content produced by drunks proved astonishing. I found an endless stream of sob stories, from teachers passing out in front of the chalkboard to farmers who vaporized entire families with a John Deere tractor.

But I located heaps of rosy profiles too. These showcased people who used to blow strangers for six-packs, kneel in their grandmother's bathroom and drink White Rain hairspray during Easter brunch, or plow through Target driving a minivan. Now clean and sober, doing stuff such as spinning their hopeful story for men and women at homeless shelters, VA hospitals, or in many cases, on long-deserted blogs. Inspiring.

My biggest takeaway took the form of smug disdain, convinced these hopeless loony birds made the way I drank look like amateur hour, making me think I jumped the gun.

But before I waffled, the sober me started soaring. I slept through the night for the first time in twenty years and greeted each morning with a clear, adrenalized point of view. One cup of coffee launched me into the stratosphere, when less than a week before, I needed two pots to untie my robe. Best of all, the stark prism I viewed the world through warmed with color, bringing the possibilities of life back in focus.

Despite these rapid advances in every imaginable aspect of my life, I couldn't bring myself to say the words out loud or in my head, *I'm never drinking again.* Perhaps a short break from drinking would do the trick, like a time-out for a hysterical child. A chance to recalibrate my body and mind, let the dust settle, and give people in my life a chance to forget why I tapped the brakes on drinking anyway.

Besides, I planned to travel back to New York one day. Soon, in fact. And I rejected the notion of outlawing my beloved long and loopy lunches at drinking holes like 21. Elbows on the bar, a martini and a plate of crab cakes, attacking a face-melting bottle of

Bordeaux. Give up autumns in New York? Historically, abandoning all sense of reason never pans out. Well, unless you're a Kardashian.

But serving two masters became a drag. Was I in or out? A moderate bore or a wretched drunk? A vegan yoga master or a wine-spilling slob passing out on the couch under a blanket of spaghetti at three in the morning? The internal friction left me numb. Then, abruptly, on one unremarkable afternoon, I committed to the idea of quitting drinking for real.

"I will never drink again," I said out loud to the mirror.

I kept this news to myself, opting out of a series of town hall meetings inside various friends and family members' homes who still bristled with disdain for me. Besides, the idea of explaining my decision and, of course, groveling for their unwanted forgiveness made me crave a drink. Bill ought to rethink step nine.

In any event, the entire population of earth figured out my dirty secret during an ordinary steak dinner with friends. When I ordered a club soda, everyone at the table froze, their faces contorted to express shock and disbelief. Did I also sense a tinge of animosity? Hard to say. But whatever they thought, if caught on film, anyone looking at the developed picture would assume my friends simultaneously caught a whiff of our waiter's trailing BO.

Their collective reaction made me flush with guilt as if I had committed a horrible crime. But in many ways, I had. Consider this: when you quit drinking, you're ripping up the social contract everybody in your life negotiated and agreed to before signing off on the terms with a feather pen dipped in red wine. No different from severing ties in any relationship, business, personal, or otherwise. In any signed contract, whoever doesn't deliver what's expected is labeled a criminal or worse. And rightfully so.

Over the next few weeks, I dragged my white knuckles everywhere I went. Dinners with friends became insufferable. Walking into cocktail parties turned into long marches of death. And if given the choice to attend a wedding or let the dentist from *Marathon Man* drill on a molar, I would open wide and say aah.

In a serendipitous fluke, I received an unexpected call from my brother. He invited me to fly down to Buenos Aires. His company secured favorable business meetings, and he figured hanging out for a few days once off the clock might be good for both of us. I agreed.

The idea of splitting town psyched me up. I also envisioned this trip would act as a brotherly solvent of sorts and help erode the thick layers of accumulated rust blocking the once-strong connection between us. As kids in California, our tight relationship blossomed and thrived. But we started growing apart before the ink on my parents' divorce papers dried. A displacing event shifting our individual survival into our sources of power.

Hampered by the mad dashes of changing states, schools, and friends (again), neither of us used our free time to nose through the how-to manual for fixing broken fraternal bonds. Because of this, if the ability to conduct a raw and vulnerable conversation classified as a talent, we wouldn't last two seconds on *The Gong Show*. Case in point: I had yet to share the scoop about my drinking.

Neither of us had spent time in Argentina. However, a hand-ful of people I admired went every year and sang the country's praises. They went to shoot dove, eat grass-fed steaks, and drink the country's legendary wines by the barrel. The highlight of every-one's trip occurred on their first morning, waking up to discover Malbec wines didn't produce the same harrowing red wine hang-overs some of us evolved to endure. They came back preaching about drinking Malbec wine all night and never having to spend the following day curled up in the fetal position on the hotel shower's floor, chewing through plastic travel packs of Aspirin like a warehouse rat.

Unquestionably, if I still drank, this divine and saucy scoop would compel me to skip naked to the airport, slinging rose petals at strangers. But my quick math determined, by the time our flight took off, I would have banged together ninety days being dry as an in-flight steak. A phenomenal fact making these corroborated field reports about Argentina's supernatural wine into some-thing less useful to me than a new embroidered vest for Grandpa Jones (RIP).

Still, my reasonable concerns persisted. Would an ocean of Malbec wine flood out of the hotel elevator doors upon arrival, like I was Danny in *The Shining*? Or did the King of Darkness run a side hustle? Maybe he oversaw a chic, boutique travel agency called Pitchfork Adventures, specializing in paradoxical vacations for abstinent nitwits like me to stress-test their recently hatched resolve. I bet a trip for the newly sober to visit the world's best city for wine became a top seller, coming in a hair behind their all-inclusive tour of Afghanistan's opium refineries aimed at junkies trying to quit smack.

My brother's business piled up cash, and he bought us first-class tickets for the overnight flight. The few times I paid to ride in first class, I covered the difference inhaling free drinks and always came out a winner, financially speaking, at least. Now, freed from the burden of compressing my budgeted travel margins, I waved off the immediate offer of complimentary champagne like the cultivated offering offended me.

Once the plane reached cruising altitude, I didn't crave a drink, a pleasant surprise since I remained glum about leaving my drinking life behind, especially now, because I held dear the elegant ritual of getting pie-eyed on long flights like this, the way a preacher thinks of baptizing a child. Did I think this sober thing through? Would I ever enjoy traveling again?

I relished my first-class seat came equipped with a private movie screen. And after scrolling through the standard titles, I selected *Mr. Woodcock*. A comic retelling of *This Boy's Life* starring Billy Bob Thornton, a movie, I supposed, guaranteed to slip me into an immediate and lasting coma.

A private car took us to the Four Seasons, arriving at the hotel during lunchtime. I spied a flock of well-dressed guests gliding into the lively café. Every patron clutched a shiny glass of wine in their hand or tapped their jeweled fingers on the polished wood of the elongated bar, waiting for another one. I purred.

After checking in, we grabbed a table for a functional lunch. An uncomplicated intake of hydrating liquids and food-based nutrients. Hampered by the noise of glasses getting refilled with savory wine and all the ginned-up laughter floating down from the bar like a bonny fog, we struggled to start a conversation. And soon, we both stared at our phones without uttering a peep. He reviewed stock prices while I investigated our airline's website, searching for the soonest flight home.

I thought about the colorful characters in *The Sun Also Rises*, saddened with jealousy about the splendid way they lived their lives. How might Hemingway describe me if I crashed his happy gang's midday saucing at a bustling café in Pamplona?

Jason's eyes were black and sad. He was not drinking. A damn fine way to waste a life. Brett teased him. "Loosen up, what a sad bore you are!" Jason grabbed his book and left. A bullfighter told me he jumped off the Pont Marie and drowned. Apagado mojado, he said. This news made me glad.

I grew dizzy anticipating my boozy moment of failure.

Once settled in our room, I cleaned up and scuttled to the gym. Afterward, I took a slow walk around the city, hoping to burn more time, which stood still when sober. When I returned to the hotel, the lobby buzzed, packed with beautiful people with broad, happy smiles, all outfitted in elegant evening clothes. Dressed for adventure. The clock said 6:00 p.m. I grimaced, regretting this trip and, more so, my hasty decision to quit drinking.

Back in the room, I found my brother stuck on a call chatting up business-related strategies and numbers, or a drug deal in Bengali for all I cared, because in my agitated condition, everything sounded like monkeys screaming at the zoo.

As we gestured loose plans around dinner, I zeroed in on the in-room bar, spellbound. Time to get the hell out. So, I hustled through the lobby, past the lively and inviting bar, thrusting beyond its gravitational tug. I picked up my pace and scooted through one of the hotel's front doors held open by a valet grinning like the devil.

The outside's warmth did little to blanket my exposed nerves. And with no city map and less time to seek directions, I shot off running like a horse whipped. In minutes, a heavy and anxious sweat, the floodwaters of sober grief, surged from my pores like a bloated kitchen sponge getting squeezed by sturdy hands.

I ran faster. And kept pushing, charged with draining the toxic fuels splashing in my tank. Finally, after an amount of time I couldn't guess, I stopped on the soft grass blanketing an urban park to catch my breath. My mind and body numbed, then started to tingle, like a phone plugged in for a recharge. Lulled by the harmonizing urban clangs and crackles of Buenos Aires, I allowed myself to jostle with the wild idea my resolve just flogged King Alcohol's fastest goon in a foot race.

Later in bed, lying on my back with my eyes closed and sucking in deep, focused breaths, I admitted to myself I liked being sober. And for the remainder of the trip, at the top of cocktail hour, I hit the streets and ran until dark, believing more with each step I meant what I said.

I appreciated spending time with my brother. Sure, we failed to crack through our emotional shells to yap about the gooey meanings of life growing inside. For instance, the discussion about my newfound sobriety, a fully flowered topic, ready to be cut up and arranged to present its maximum value, ended quick, as considerable as a passerby's belch. The spoken equivalent of two white guys attempting a high five. Another enduring reminder of our Midwestern stock.

I respected myself for not stubbing my toe on the bar's steps and treating the rest of the trip like a bigger and better sequel to the black-and-white experimental art-house flop I made in Montana. And so, as prehistoric cave dwellers at last learned to lick fire burned their woolly lips, I realized being sober provided the most sensible way for me to stay alive.

Back home, all the encouraging clichés about sobriety came true. I lost weight, I did better at work, and my cheeks stopped looking like two ripe apples. But after a few months, sobriety's manic shine faded after I shifted my focus on things yet to change for the better.

Bills kept coming, cars continued to get flats, and I remained mixed on how to thank my neighbor for training his dogs to bark through the night: tip off local meth cooks when he went on vacation or burn his house to the ground with a military-grade blowtorch.

I understood the jagged rhythm of mania better than most. So, when aggravating things remained aggravating, I chose indifference. But to my intensifying disappointment, Lucia and I continued turning commonplace conversations about petty nonsense into elaborate and nasty arguments about everything. These silly dustups were common when I drank and were quickly blamed on wine. Now, being sober, our regular matrimonial conflicts escalated into all-out wars. Heartbreaking. Because once I tossed the bottle, I thought every stupid reason to fight went out the window with it. So now, anytime we got into a row, it confused me more than the climax of *The Sixth Sense*.

Additionally, my decision to quit drinking received less than trace amounts of meaningful support from other adults in my life, who chose to recognize my efforts by deleting my contact information from their phones or keeping their physical distance altogether, like I flaunted symptoms linked to yellow fever. And on the rare occasions when they couldn't avoid me, I got to bask in their leery contempt, like they thought I might start pitching cheap soap and margarine for Amway. In every case, nobody stopped drinking long enough to ask me how I felt, what kept me busy, or if I wanted to play golf.

I overheard a dear friend (a legendary drinker in his own right) say to a group of my other dear friends, "Hey, I'm proud of him. I mean, if anyone needed to quit, Jason did."

I didn't need or expect support from my friends. But at the same time, how would Dolly Parton respond if the only support from her closest friends came when they pitched in and bought her a training bra?

Inside, a frosty hostility worked its way into the cracks of my goodwill and expanded. I started pulling away from adults, spending my free time training for a marathon, and hanging out with my kids.

Now sober, fully engaged, and ever-present, our time together became a waking dream. And through my kids, I discovered an untapped source of power and strength, generated by the miracle of them never having to suffer living with the man I almost became and how they survived unscathed, showing no signs of lasting damage left behind by my boozy storms of the past.

Of course, through the advancement of technology, the more we've come to understand storms, they're still impossible to predict. So, nine months after I quit drinking, when the Cabernet tsunami wiped me out, I found myself ill-equipped to move forward.

After a few primitive digs through the rubble, I failed to locate signs of my sober life pinned beneath. My bootless efforts required more than man's earthly competence could muster, especially on his own. As a result, I committed myself to drinking again, vowing to go the distance this time, unburdened of reason's drag.

CLASS ACT

oinciding with the coked-up apex of mid-'80s glamour and greed and brimming with less hope than an escaped prisoner of war, an invigorating but illogical complement propelled me to keep crawling through seventh grade's hawkish muck. I listened dumbstruck as friends, strangers, and the occasional breathless middle-aged pervert cruising the arcade pointed out I looked like Rob Lowe.

More preposterous, the ink-smeared school paper validated the story in a celebrity look-alike list. A blurb the teachers patched together, I suspected, as a farce or tasked to a student keen to learn the publishing process despite being legally blind.

Simultaneously, I bristled at flattery, long conditioned to treat arbitrary upticks in self-worth by inducing Munchausen-grade sarcasm.

Funny. Most people say Curtis Armstrong!

Besides, mirrors reflected my harsh truth. Saddled with a face galloping through acne, stabled under a thatched bed of scruffy brown hair still spooked by the sight of Vidal Sassoon mousse. And because of my braces, which made the orthodontic hardware Richard Kiel wore in *Moonraker* invisible, I stopped smiling, and my dimples (an actual strength) shriveled under to rot. Not exactly cover-boy material for *Teen Beat* or *Bop*.

But on the inside, the defiant remains of my unsullied promise beamed. Being mistaken for Sodapop Curtis from *The Outsiders*? I found no harm in running this hallucinatory comparison right through the earth's core and decided to lean into these iffy comparisons to Mr. Lowe. In fact, I signed up for saxophone lessons at the local college after *St. Elmo's Fire* lathered every girl on earth up into a horn-blowing frenzy.

During the first lesson, the instructor, a failed musician, explained playing the saxophone in basic terms, pointing out things like the reed and the neck and telling me if I dedicated the rest of my life to the instrument and practiced for a billion hours, I might make a total of twenty dollars playing street corners before hawking the horn at a pawn shop and getting just enough to cover a bus ticket home and a dime bag of tar. So, about ten minutes into the first six lessons, I checked out, choosing to withhold the about-face from my mom as a protective buffer between her current hope and eventual disappointment.

When she dropped me off for the following five lessons, I scampered to the student union to drink fountain Cokes and survey the stunning college girls wearing denim skirts and neon T-shirts embroidered with Greek letters. Of course, not a single coed beauty approached me, breathless and trembling, twisting her white Reeboks through the floor, too flushed to ask me for an autograph or gush over my career-solidifying performance in *Class Act*.

Even so, I paid close attention to Rob Lowe's career and rooted for his success. And why not? The more his angelic face fronted the cover of trashy magazines, the better chance a random oddball might toss me a rotten chunk of vacant praise, like I was a stilted seal prancing for mackerel after bouncing a beach ball off my nose.

But the day Rob's fresh-faced mug beautified every front page in America, sensationalizing his role in a steamy three-way at the '88 Democratic National Convention, my world started to crumble. I ignored the pundits condemning Lowe's character and dismissed his curious support for Michael Dukakis.

Instead, my immediate focus swirled around the lingering possibility of Rob Lowe getting blackballed out of show business and forever labeled an undesirable creep or, worse, becoming a permanent fixture on *Hollywood Squares*.

You see, kids, before Facebook made doppelgänger an actual word, mine lived on the fast track leading to international stardom.

Now Hollywood's top train controller might flip his track's switch, putting his career on the same eastbound rail tasked with hauling the likes of Bert Convy and James Brolin to Branson, Missouri, relegating them to the unscripted variety shows staged in play-houses famous for their pork ribs.

In other words, the next time anyone mixed me up with Rob Lowe (outside the Ozarks) would occur once Leif Garrett ruled Broadway. But to my relief, in less than a month, nobody cared. Tragedy avoided. God Bless America.

Much later in college, I read Rob Lowe passed the ten-year mark measuring his sobriety. And before the internet exploited a celebrity's every waking moment, his milestone constituted meaningful news, at least to me.

Likewise, around the same time, another talented actor I admired, Jason Bateman, came out as sober. It surprised me a fluff piece in *Us Weekly* would lead me to think, much less ruminate, on the contextual parallels of the subject's life with mine. But since I grew up watching Bateman blow Ricky Schroder out of every shared scene in *Silver Spoons* before lighting up his own path to riches with the shine coming off the short-lived gem *It's Your Move*, the article packed a contemplative punch.

Naturally, like any legitimate child actor, his flame got pinched out before learning to shave. And he spent the next twenty years pinballing his Range Rover off parked cars all over LA, while his career choices whittled down to dubious roles in garbage like *Teen Wolf Too*.

But he decided to stop boozing. And right away, the quality of his life and the roles being offered trended up, starting with his masterful work in *Arrested Development*. And punctuated by adding heft to lightweight comedies like *The Break-Up* and *Dodgeball* in throwaway roles. *That's good clean fun, eh, Cot?*

Often, I fantasized about a world where my family didn't implode back in third grade. And instead of getting dragged out of Laguna Hills kicking and screaming, I made an earnest attempt at becoming a child actor. In this scenario, Jason Bateman and I would've run around town in similar circles. And as sure as Dana Plato would snort another line, we'd become best friends. The two Jasons!

Soon, in this alternate reality, my career picked up after dazzling power players in a plum role on a doomed sitcom, *Boy Bites Dog!* Before solidifying my acting chops in a guest part on *The Love Boat*, playing a dimple-cheeked preteen Lothario (an unhinged stalker by today's standards) with the hot sweats for Julie.

If only you were twenty years older, Timmy.

And don't forget rich!

Isaac, that's terrible!

Buoyed by postshow buzz, I moved up the actors' food chain, starring in A-list child roles, like the overwhelmed and baffled kid in *Kramer vs. Kramer*. Followed up by playing the kid in *The Black Stallion*, who was also overwhelmed and baffled.

Life in this world only got dreamier. For instance, at my tenth birthday party, hosted by my dirtbag agent at his art deco drug den carved out of Laurel Canyon, I met Drew Barrymore. After opening my presents, Drew and I snorted up our first fat line of LA's best blow before sharing our first innocent kiss. Aw. Sniff, sniff.

Fast-forward to nine years later. I'm standing in a seedy drug dealer's living room, getting sprayed down by an Uzi for trying to sell his crew two pounds of off-brand powdered coffee creamer as yayo, a scene years later reprised to eerie perfection in *Boogie Nights*. Pop! Pop! Pop!

As always, in my alternate universe (trivial movie role fluctuations aside), the conclusive climax of my flameout fairy tale made Danny Bonaduce's epic collapse in real life play out more wholesome than *The Muppet Show*'s Christmas special.

I envied Bateman's new awakening. He spoke with comfortable confidence and projected a bewildering sense of gratitude while keeping his outlook on the future measured and in check with his signature deadpan retorts, making his renaissance seem real.

Now, aged forty-two, back in the real world, and about to drive my family home after spending the week loitering along the Florida coast. A joyful week highlighted by decent waves, plenty of sunshine, and getting admonished by multiple bartenders for trying to order Patron shots after fast-fisting five Malbecs down the hatch. *The more you know...*

Of course, Lucia was livid. I deserved whatever coming wrath accompanied the long drive home. But before we left, on a whim, I downloaded the audio version of Rob Lowe's book, *Stories I Only Tell My Friends*. I figured Rob Lowe's audiobook would provide me needed air cover from Lucia's impending attacks.

Imagine. Endless loads of steamy gossip, tawdry bedroom recaps, and hopefully an overdue explanation around the inexplicable reasons he dated Melissa Gilbert. All the scintillating ear candy would help keep her mesmerized and quiet, allowing me to kick the can down the road once again. Ideally, all the way to Texas.

Above all, Rob Lowe's depraved Brat Pack fables would normalize my own rueful behavior, providing me with narrative evidence I planned on triple wrapping in conjecture before presenting my case to the jury with exaggerated virtue and a knowing wink.

Your honor, if I may, I will now read aloud the second to last paragraph from the chapter in Mr. Lowe's book titled, "Only If It Walked."

After all, like every other woman on earth, my wife's heart would stop beating at the sound of Rob's raspy and blameless voice, and all the hate Lucia developed for me would melt to mush, no matter what he talked about. And let's be honest, what else is Rob Lowe deputized to discuss besides all the chicks he banged, all the booze he drank, and all the blow he snorted off Ally Sheedy's ass during the production of *Oxford Blues*? I planned to exit my vehicle after the long drive, looking like an irreproachable saint.

However, only a few minutes in, this audiobook revealed itself to be a spoiler to my hopeful expectations. Nothing like the down and dirty tell-all I purchased to whitewash my character. He didn't even speak the way I expected—vacant and sheepish.

And this "book" didn't come off anything like a saucy cash grab, like Rob dictated his musings into a recording app strolling barefoot along Leadbetter Beach, anything to kill time between his impending romp with a thong model.

Quite the opposite. His story sounded touching and profound, anchored by an inspiring (if not unnerving) degree of humility I never expect from anyone, much less from a man so seriously, ridiculously good-looking. Worst of all, Mr. Lowe happens to be a damn fine writer, which minimized whatever petty jealousies I harbored for lacking his handsome features down to a passive speck.

The book failed to gloss over my failings as a drinker and man. But coincidently, Rob Lowe and I do share common traits besides our, um, appearance. A few things, in fact. We both brimmed with metric tons of self-doubt, lugged around father issues of a Midwestern kind, and possessed a reluctant capacity to understand a particular style of drinking only ends one way.

To that end, he dedicated one chapter to describe, with meticulous bone-chilling detail, the backend of his worst hangover. The fateful day started with an early morning phone call, jolting him awake like a cattle prod (my description). That's when he learned his grandfather, the only man genuinely close to him, died.

He hung up the phone, shocked. Laid out in a hotel room like a bloated corpse dredged up from the bottom of a Machado Lake, all alone, heartbroken, and sad in ways he never imagined possible. I mean, he was the biggest star in the world. Life goes on, right? How bad can living be when a supermodel holding coke stands naked waiting behind every bedroom door?

He grabbed a half-full bottle of tequila from his bedside table, intent on guzzling down every drop in one breath. But he froze and stared at the bottle for an amount of time he couldn't recall. Gazing at the sweetest relief imaginable floating inside, waving him in, as amiable and trusting as Richard Dawson on *Family Feud*, before a miracle shook him, and he put the bottle down for good.

Using clean and confident brushstrokes, he painted a moving portrait of his life after booze. With zero traces of self-loathing, regret, or smug judgment, the rest of the book laid out an elegant blueprint for a life powered by love and contagious gratitude. Oh, and without booze, his career kind of took off. Turns out he was seriously, ridiculously talented too.

His book ruffled me, changing the way I thought about everything. I started considering the history of my drinking behavior. At dinner parties, did everyone end up blackout drunk like me? I always assumed so and quickly excused my deplorable conduct.

Now, watching *Seinfeld*, I realized Jerry and his friends, blessed with the gift of unlimited time from doing nothing, found things to do besides day-drink their way through every wine bar on the Upper West Side, which was as unimaginable to me as running a four-minute mile or…

Without alcohol, at least for Rob Lowe, life blossomed. Essential human needs and priorities bubbled up and flowed downstream, away from all the rocks and rapids, keeping him afloat, steady, in the river's deepest, most centered current, the best place to spot all the miracles waving from the banks.

What are the odds? Rob Lowe, my childhood idol and, ahem, pretty-boy doppelgänger, prompted me to think about drinking in a way that made me hate myself more. In my mind, sobriety transformed from an unconnected word into the most alluring mirage.

And as I drove homeward in the dark, I visualized (or hallucinated, whatever) a flamenco dancer on the hood of my car, ablaze in a red dress, draped in blinding jewels, grinning with lips too angelic to kiss. Radiant and magnificent, seducing me to join her on the grand ballroom's clear, see-through floor, which she hovered over like a clairvoyant, loving ghost visiting to resolve my drunken past and lead me to where I wanted to be and curse my life to hell, where God created me to be.

Grab my hand, sweet child.

I can't remember if some bootlicking cowboy driving a Dodge Ram with Oklahoma plates veered into my lane, nearly running me off the road, or I plowed over a pothole deep enough for bears to soak in, but something caused me to jump out of my skin, and the beautiful dancer before my eyes vanished in a defeated flash.

With ten more hours of road to endure, I convinced myself Rob Lowe's miraculous tale stunk like a hearty bowl of Hollywood mumbo jumbo. No more than a slick fantasy meant to be approximated only after leveraging a willing suspension of disbelief. Assuming the same delusional state of mind to accept his character in *St. Elmo's Fire* (Billy the freeloading Lothario who faked playing the sax) retained enough brain cells to graduate from Georgetown.

Sobriety reads well on paper and sounds better recited with Rob Lowe's attractive voice. But in my previously failed and unsupported attempts to break away from alcohol's long reach, my brain suffered permanent damage. To believe in beating King Alcohol's war machine required a lobotomy, or whatever kind of detached voodoo curse the casting director on *St. Elmo's Fire* fell under to think offering the role of Wendy Beamish to Mare Winningham would pan out.

The biggest lesson from the book, at least to me, since I didn't resemble anything close to the seriously, ridiculously good-looking guy in the first place, is I'd be a fool to continue thinking we shared a single thing in common.

Lucky for me, Thanksgiving was around the corner. My favorite time of the year to recalibrate my life around all I'm grateful for.

TURDS OF A
FEATHER

Thanksgiving is my favorite holiday. More enjoyable to me than discovering a shiny pile of undeserved presents jammed under the tree on Christmas morning, I grew up preferring the earthy tones and languid pace associated with Turkey Day, starting with better food, football, and thanks to the day's ever-present clangs coming from the kitchen, the realistic hope my dad's conspicuous daytime boozing would go unnoticed like grease dissolving in gravy.

Even better, one of my uncles tended to hog most of the unwanted attention to himself. For example, one year, when I was seven, my uncle reached into the center of the table, snagged the butter plate like money found, and plopped the dish in front of his overstuffed plate. Then he nabbed a piping hot cob of corn, mashed it across the stick of butter, and started spinning it, reminding me of a nubby tire stuck in slick mud.

Now awestruck, made dizzy by the utilitarian genius of his modernized basting process, I ogled him in an opportunistic daze, the way a caveman would stare, mouth agape, at a laser gun or a three-pronged dildo.

I didn't pick up the room's vibe downshifting into funeral-wake territory, nor did my uncle, who kept spinning his corn in a book-ish stupor, with all the self-awareness of a vodka-crocked Russian manning a lathe.

Excited, I waited my turn. But the room's sudden silence caught my attention. Papo, whose opinion on all matters I trusted most, stared daggers of scorn through my woolgathering uncle, still happy as a pig rolling in slick slop. The other grown-ups studied him too. Regretful and annoyed, united by their sizzling contempt.

Meanwhile, still oblivious to our loving family's disdainful wrath, my uncle squished another corncob on the spin cycle. I took one last look and closed my eyes, pausing to mark the gratitude that stemmed from not following his lead.

Don't ever be Thanksgiving's biggest asshole, I vowed.

Thirty years later, Lucia and I delighted in carving out Thanksgiving traditions of our own. We agreed on creating a

Turkey Day experience our kids would relish and grow up inspired to pay the gift forward to their own.

Our modest intentions didn't involve recreating the cover of the *Saturday Evening Post*. But if my kids took a true-or-false quiz about Thanksgiving and checked the "true" box at least twice, I would die satisfied knowing we exceeded our reasonable holiday objectives.

THE CARTER FAMILY
THANKSGIVING SURVEY

- True or False: You're eager to introduce extended family members to your friends from school.

- True or False: When you evaluate members of your extended family, you think, *Gosh, they're the best.*

- True or False: People often comment that the chummy relationship between your dad and brother-in-law reminds them of Zach Braff and Donald Faison on *Scrubs*.

- True or False: When the Macy's Parade comes on, you don't shoot the television with a shotgun.

To amplify our efforts, we made a tradition of spending the long weekend at my wife's family's sizable, brush-country ranch an hour south of San Antonio. Their spread boasted wide-open spaces and endless horizons in every direction, all held together by an old-school lodge often mentioned by fun-loving people well versed in the art of wild nights in South Texas.

As usual, we left San Antonio on Wednesday afternoon and headed south. In addition to tons of food, pets, and my family, I brought along my own lofty aspiration—to reconnect with the concept of gratitude. In doing so, I hoped to find cause to slow down my drinking, which, in the past six months, had found more power, hissing past apex status like a bottle rocket, and kept zooming into the cosmos.

I'm sad to report I woke up Thursday morning riddled with confusion, having no idea how or when I got to bed the night before. All magnified through a special lens invented to uncover hidden brutes of shame prowling inside the still-drunk mind.

The usual pain, shame, and crushing remorse knotted inside my whopping hangovers yielded to an unaffected purr of self-righteousness. Who in my presence dares to judge? Not that I found grounds to care.

Lucia's conspicuous absence from our bedroom didn't help. As a matter of fact, her side of the bed remained untouched, but somewhere in the house, she fumed so much my eyes stung, like tear gas rushed under the door. Madder than hell. Not at me. Or the way I drank. But now, I recognized, madder than hell for being my wife. And who could blame her? I was one unexpected Christmas party in Palm Springs away from becoming Julian in *Less Than Zero*.

But seconds before revoking my gratitude search, I perked up, remembering today was Thanksgiving. A day when Bloody Marys and chilled wine flowed fast and heavy all day from sunup to man down, without consequence.

Elated, beyond grateful, I popped out of bed and took a hot shower. Once scrubbed clean and damp with a citrus sandalwood cologne, I waltzed toward the sounds of the new day's action but stopped, fearful of the sadistic reception awaiting my emergence on the main stage. My powdery mouth wetted with dread, pasting it closed, fearing my next steps like a Kurdish rebel before singing "Mawtini" in front of Saddam Hussein.

The show goes on, I reminded myself before taking the first step out.

I spotted my father-in-law sitting by the bar, glass in his hand. And my stage fright vanished in one breath, replaced by the hand-wrought faith found in desert troubadours, sanctioning them to conceive their sandy song voice sounds like Luciano Pavarotti. In any case, my fortunes turned.

That's because Lucia's dad is king, the family's regulator of law and order. Translation: When the king drinks, I drink. So, empowered by the intoxicating freedom of diplomatic immunity, I pimp-walked to the bar and dropped in the chair next to him, bracing myself for takeoff.

"What are you having?" I asked.

"Coffee," he replied, dejected, like telling me his bones tingled with cancer.

I almost fainted from shock. Could I be passed out and having a nightmare? I never hoped for more.

His wife traipsed by, using her stunning blue eyes to flash him the stink eye of torrid spousal discontent, a visual reflex common in wives with husbands who guzzled up a blizzard the night before and, like me, were banished to rot out the day on Dry Island. Or else.

We sat in grim silence, falling into a tense standoff of sorts. We shifted our eyeballs between a clock on the wall and the shining bottles of liquor and chilled wine mocking us from the top of the bar.

On a relatable note, as a kid, I subscribed to *Boy's Life*. I read an article about prisoners of war subject to days of torture if caught uttering a peep.

They learned to suffer in silence, but over time, in their case years, they adapted to their unfitting environment. And their sensory neurons evolved, enabling the men to communicate by sharing thoughts. From a scientific perspective, our imprisonment situation proved to be a billion times worse. Because the evolutionary timeline to develop telepathic powers didn't stretch past five minutes before we started reading each other's minds.

We both thought getting the first drink of the day, at this hour, in these hostile conditions, held fatal. Doing so, we agreed silently, required the strategic intuition of a Russian chess master tied around the frenzied intentions of a suicide bomber.

But unfortunately, between the two of us, we didn't command the right stuff, and we concluded, in clairvoyant unison, to lay down our guns.

Then a holiday miracle happened. A welcome guest came breezing in. A dashing and delightful woman from a prominent South Texas family—dressed for lunch at Neiman's and glowing with anticipation—resurrected my thirsty spirit's lust for mischief. She stopped, peering down at Lucia's dad and me, curious and bemused.

"What are you two dummies waiting for, an engraved invitation?"

She motioned me to uncork the bottle of Chardonnay sitting on ice. And didn't wave off my pour until the titillating wine kissed the top of her glass's rim.

"Happy Thanksgiving, indeed!" she said, floating out of the room like Ginger Rogers boarding a yacht.

My father-in-law and I exchanged a disbelieving glance, both speechless. What followed went down as the most incredible three-day holiday bender performed by a man. For me, at least. In terms of volume, velocity, and sheer doggedness, this binge zoomed past my booziest bouts in college and the subsequent two decades of blackout bachelor parties, weddings, and the countless weekends sunk to the bottom of the ocean by trying to drink it.

The ensuing week, as winter skies turned pitch black each day before lunchtime, I sank into a deep depression. My list of causes stretched long. Topping the list were my children: Holden, Richard, and Ruby. Ages eleven, ten, and six. Each of my beautiful little miracles proved observant enough to store experiences, including the most granular and gory bits related to dad's boozing into infinity with the infallible permanence of a Pentagon server.

Making matters worse, I understood, better than most, certain types of memories can scramble a child's brain in a click, faster than fleshy smut crashes an office network when the VP of Sales downloads porn.

Running this binary I/O through my own pickle-brained hard drive exposed my most profound fear—turning into Thanksgiving's biggest asshole. At this point, the only thing keeping me undecided spilled out from a bottle.

So, on December 1, sitting in the Men's Grill at San Antonio Country Club draining my third Styrofoam cup of "a double Goose with a splash," my prolonged infatuation with finding peaceful ground conceded to my desire to destroy it.

"Curtis, another, please," I said to the bartender.

OUT OF FIN AIR

ix days removed from describing the manic details of my make-believe suicide to a psychiatrist with the smug nonchalance of Warren Beatty pitching an autobiographical script at the Ivy, I cringed and cursed myself for blathering on about killing myself like a lunatic to a total stranger.

The guardians of remorse tossed me into countless black holes. And I always clawed my way out, and we both moved on. Isn't that how relationships worked? Only this time, alcohol's guilty gears ground me down to blood gravy, using enough torque to hoist a prison bus out of a swamp. But ending my life? Because of drinking? Hell, Brandon Walsh from the early days of *90210* thought I overreacted.

For my time and $350, I received the groundbreaking advice to dial back my drinking, a prescription for Lamictal, and her diagnosis branding me as an unsalvageable, piping hot, bipolar mess. Thanks for playing. I derived more satisfaction from losing my wallet or paying a predatory tow truck driver the same amount to unhook my car from his crooked hitch.

At any rate, I classified my rambling monologue detailing a belly flop off a specific bridge as a feverish one-off. Nothing more than a childish reaction to the boogeyman from an average Joe winded from three decades of warring with pitch-black depression, which only retreated when I fired back with a flurry of drinks. Nothing to see here.

Besides, I hadn't touched a drop since. And my skin glowed like a table lamp. So, for this reason, after a magical day on the slopes with my wife and kids, and one nanosecond after showering and getting dressed, I ditched my family and shuffled over to a wine bar on the west side of town for a nip of slippery *rojo* to punctuate this terrific day and my elevated mood.

I drank a few afternoon reds at this place the year before and remembered chatting with the bartender. A New Yorker. She told me she came to Telluride on a girls' trip and decided to stay. If I recall, she quit her job on Wall Street and purchased the bar. Whatever the case, she met the best version of herself in Telluride and planted a stake in the ground.

I remember admiring her because if we're not spending every second of our fleeting lives doing what we love, the only air worth breathing is in a closed garage, sitting in an idling 1976 Trans Am with no muffler while "Sister Christian" plays at full blast. A sensible mandate I agreed with but lacked the courage to act on.

Of course, she might be long gone. Back to New York after a long and lonesome winter during which she came unglued shoveling the obligatory Subaru she acquired out of chest-deep snow. Perhaps she longed for her old doorman's toothy smile and endless babble. Both of which—when she called the building where he worked home and obliged to withstand his dopey observations five times during a typical day—she hated his guts for. I bet her shiny idealism got covered in spring mud after realizing a Colorado bagel compared to a New York bagel equated to wearing a burlap sack instead of the $9,000 spider silk pajamas approved by Goop's Gwyneth Paltrow. *Wearing them makes me so horny!*

Regardless, I set my course westward. Indifferent about whatever enlightened person escaped reality to pour my wine. As I made my way at a brisk clip, unprovoked, my intense hankering for a drink atomized into a mist of inanimate and metallic matter before regenerating into ferocious intent. My movements became machinelike, rigid, and efficient. Now void of emotion and unstoppable, like a T-1000 bearing down on the aloof twit mucking up judgment day.

But when I got to the wine bar, instead of pouring through cracks in the wall like white-hot metal, I paused and peered inside. No sign of the bartender from New York. This bugged me. Primarily because in her place stood the type of bearded, smug-faced hipster jerkoff who drives agreeable people like me to despise everything about Colorado, including bluegrass music and handcrafted beer.

Now, anything I ordered came with the considerable risk of getting looped into an irritating conversation. The looming threat of sitting through another phony bartender's hand-me-down life story in exchange for a spicy buzz would cost me more than I valued life itself.

I dreamt of becoming an IP lawyer in Seattle. But the movie Into the Wild *came out. And here I am!*

Fuming, I launched into a finicky march to nowhere, heading to the end of town with no plan or purpose. The only noise came from the debating voices in my head.

One glass? Keep walking. One glass? Keep walking.

I continued moving west, dazed, listening to the spirited fight play out in my mind, like a hard-fought point in tennis.

One glass? Keep walking. One glass? Keep walking, asshole!

The point's abrupt end. A screaming backhand winner stopped by the back wall, followed by roars and cheers from the crowd, which buffered down to a smattering of stately applause and, finally, silence.

The balmy spring mountain temperature dropped in a snap, giving the air icy teeth and a bite, startling me out of my head and back into waking life. My stride picked up, rapid but graceless and flush with agitation, like a weary traveler racing through a terminal late for a flight.

Finally, I stopped walking. After taking in a sequence of knotty deep breaths, I glimpsed around. I stood alone on a quiet neighborhood street. Isolated from all the hapless tourists picking up T-shirts and lip balm or blowing what chairlift operators make in a year on custom leather jackets stitched together by a subversive local artist getting economic revenge.

It was getting late. The dimming sun already dissolving into the towering mass of the San Juan Mountains turned the sky red, orange, and pink.

About a block ahead, I spotted a small bench sitting in a yard. My body turned heavy and sluggish. I trudged to the bench and sat down, which provided no relief. Every part of me still ached. The long drive up, followed by two full days of skiing down the mountain, left me ragged.

But soon, my bones softened and squished through the seat as the color drained from my shadowy thoughts, staining the demons dawdling in my twitchy head black. Next, as the sky above me shifted and streaked in a way I recalled seeing once before but couldn't place where or when, my thick eyelids dashed down to an abrupt stop, unable to move, resting like felled stage curtains in an abandoned playhouse.

After a hushed minute, spectral images of my life started flickering in front of me, projected onto a screen close enough to touch. Then, in a vivid gush, the prism's colors washed over the scene as if proudly announcing the film utilized Technicolor technology.

In the opening scene, the nine-year-old me sat in the back of a Corolla. My young face appeared blank as I gazed out the window. I remembered this moment so well. When I got dragged away from my meaningful life in California right after my parents' marriage exploded. The grim thought of starting from scratch carving out the soft parts of my heart and brain.

The montage continued: Guzzling down my first beer on the farm. Smoking a Winston. Throwing up an orange flood of guts after discovering the magic inside California Coolers. Keeping kegs company on the beach and in backyards. My first bottle of wine. Wild parties in high school and college. Cursing a blue streak in front of Lucia's parents. Stumbling through subway stations in New York at four in the morning. Falling on dance floors inside roped-off clubs in LA. Hunched in front of my laptop, glassy-eyed with purple lips stained by cheap wine. Opening the door to my dad's place after he died, stunned by the prodigious collection of empty bourbon bottles littering the floor. Inhaling scotch at my wedding reception. Arguing with my wife near the bar (of course) at a party. Passed out on a riverbank in Montana. Slurring to my kids. Thanksgiving. Slumping on the couch inside the Men's Grill at the Country Club, staring down at melted ice and vodka with black, lifeless eyes, ordering another.

The next scene took longer to play out. I was jogging over a skyway under the same kind of mesmerizing sky above me now. I stopped running, paused, took in a deep breath, and jumped, with no reflective pause. The camera didn't pan down, and the sounds of my skin smacking the cement and the immediate, soupy explosion of my body getting splattered by a speeding truck remained off-screen.

Now a young boy again, wide-eyed and innocent and in a dreamy trance, watching *Cosmos* at my neighbors' house, back when I lived in Southern California. What the...? I sprang off the floor like someone snapped my back with a wet towel.

"Fuck you!" my dad screamed.

He morphed into a grotesque beast, making the original monster from *Alien* resemble a bunny sniffing at a plate of strawberries. No physical semblance of my dad, the man I worshiped and loved, remained.

"It's all shit. Fuck you!"

My boyish face turned to stone. And in a white flash, I transformed into an unrecognizable version of myself. The same way Luke saw his dark side while tripping balls with Yoda on planet Dagobah. Or how Corey Feldman sees himself every day.

This breezy sequence from my childhood shocked me out of the movie, stunning me from the ability to continue watching, leaving me breathless and disturbed in the most melodramatic way.

As I mellowed, I recalled the famous gotcha moments in films like *The Sixth Sense*, when Bruce Willis figured out, finally, he's the underworld's dumbest ghost. A situational circumstance I always thought any idiot would piece together in the first act trying to hail a cab. Or when Dil, the beautiful and alluring sexpot in *The Crying Game*, whipped out her sizable dong.

Was the *Cosmos* incident a visceral plant in my own movie that paid off by exposing the moment my adolescence vanished without a trace? The scene when I got popped senseless with a hammer and dragged into an unmarked white van, rushed to a dark basement, and tortured to death before they sawed my body up, double-bagged the bones and flesh, and tossed my soupy remains in a landfill to rot?

Or was another scene coming when my mom giggled at my dad's curious statement and playfully threw a cream pie in his face? Then we all cracked up. Until, of course, a flurry of pies started flying in from everywhere and smashing into our own faces. Pie fight! The action stopped abruptly, though, when a plump man entered the room.

Did someone order a box of pies?

Dom DeLuise! What are you doing here?

But before a vaudevillian pie fight erupted, the images on the screen melted bright white, like the film caught on fire, blinding me, making me squint. I sat in the dark, a little uneasy about the scenes chosen to spotlight my life's linear narrative leading me to this precise point in a universe where time isn't measured but swallowed up into black holes, like life itself never existed.

Tears formed in my eyes, bubbling out and lagging downward before picking up speed, like growing white balls of snow rolling down a mountain before hurling off the edge of my flushed cheeks, splattering on the ground.

I came unhooked from organic life. Now free-falling beyond

the speed of fleshy physics, like I was a chunk of osmium tied to a boat motor. But my mind settled, releasing an extraordinary wave of peace, which washed over my twitchy nerves. I had never sampled such a pleasurable nothingness so transcendental albeit deeply rooted to the earth's core, like an inexplicable state of beingness clawing its way through the restrictive walls of mortality, hell-bent on finding a place eclipsing the most poetic definition of the biological paragon.

Daring to believe the uninfluenced serenity familiar to bear cubs stuffed with elk meat and berries when they sleep between their parents' well-heated, furry bodies exists and is Goddamn gettable.

All the sharp cerebral carvings marking my brain like a potluck ham at a funeral wake smeared into blemishes and blots. And the decades of toxic emotional sludge I held inside heated up to a boil, creating the steam and pressure needed to blast open a steel box. I wanted to sob but couldn't draw a breath.

You don't have to do this anymore.

I gazed up at the sky and the mountains. Moonbeams and sun streaks lit up the valley the way fireworks trumpet a grand finale. An explosive showcase prophetic of endings and finality, the universal declaration stating things are wrapping up. And soon, all remaining are agitated parents corralling sleepy kids to cars, scads of litter, and the infinite darkness of my own world's demise.

I found air and sucked my lungs full. Enough to stretch the tightness out of my chest and blow out an exhausted howl, sounding like the last call of a wolf expiring, stuck in a faceless hunter's bone-crushing claw trap. Robbed of his ability to run or fight, only a few withering senses remained to soak up the lethal frequencies pulsating off the woodsman's approach as the wired tendons of his firing hand wrapped around the trigger of a high-powered rifle.

You don't have to do this anymore.

I mashed my face in my hands and swayed back and forth. In the darkness, behind my closed eyes pressed hard against my hands, millions of colors and oscillating shapes swirled in an infinite depth, pulling me into another dimension. In this cosmic realm, the sound of familiar words played on a loop, as if spoken to me before, many times, in fact, starting as a child.

You don't have to do this anymore.

But the words always sounded too muffled to understand. As if the sound waves hauling them emitted from another world and traveled through the equivalent of a thousand sandstorms to reach me, only to find me doing slow-motion flips underwater or rocking out to Van Halen at full blast.

Only now, after slicing through the clutter with, I can only assume, infuriated exasperation, they sounded distinct and pressing, like the messenger realized his cell was muted this whole time for the last thirty years.

You don't have to do this anymore!

The definitive statement grabbed me like the sturdy hands belonging to a farmer's wife, warm and strong, squeezing me tight, not at all hurtful, only deliberately, with a practical purpose, to ring the filth out of me the way she might handle her husband's best white shirt, soiled after chasing down a runaway hog spotted driving home from church together in their pea-green Buick.

Startled by the sound of an opening door, which, in my loopy fog, sounded more like detonating avalanche dynamite, I jumped to attention, finding myself shaking, with every nerve in my system exposed and on high alert.

Out of the door walked a short and scruffy man dragging an aluminum can full of trash. He stopped and smiled. We studied each other. He stared deep through my eyes and nodded, glad to meet me. I shook my head up and down like a fool. He held his gaze long enough to perceive tear streaks on my face.

His face softened, contorting to relay the message hinting that life will be okay, like whatever placed me in front of him—sobbing like Ricky Schroder as Jon Voight bled out at the end of *The Champ* —he expected.

He walked around the corner of the house, dragging the trash can behind him, causing the metal to grind against the cement. An annoying sound to most but one with a history of making me come unglued. But not here. Not now. This scratchy friction sounded almost musical, like an experimental art-house band trying to play an eccentric melody of hope after dabbing out. Within the tune lived an untrained, dogged purity oscillating in the song's undercurrent, leading me to believe the better notes would reward my patience.

But the grating noise failed to evolve, only faded out and disappeared, reminding me of hearing the opening synth notes of Van Halen's "Jump" for the first time in seventh grade. Going from hopeful to exasperated in six seconds flat before descending into madness until the song's blessed end.

After the man and the noise vanished, the world remained silent, much like the crowds attending David Lee Roth's concerts promoting his solo career.

I never hurt so much to be surrounded by my kids. I wanted to sprint back to the condo to wrap my arms around them and never let go. In a heightened state, I stood up and began my way toward them. The sun set, but the vivid moon's brilliant glow made the world brighter by a thousand suns.

A small creek gurgled nearby, and for a flash, the water sounded loud and violent, more like a raging river crashing against giant rocks. My sight blurred with tears, forcing me to wipe my eyes before finding a smooth part of the road to walk.

You don't have to do this anymore.

The affecting tone of the cryptic voice changed. No longer melodic and celestial, its peculiar and transmutable pitch now sounded dry and specific, familiar even. Not unlike me and the tone I'd use telling a friend to quit a job they hated or stop using a trendy laxative causing them full-body cramps and uncontrollable gas.

To me, the updated, plainspoken manner emphasized in the frank and understated tenor revealed its judicial roots, arming the axiom with terrestrial credibility, which made hearing the words more freeing, as if a respectable, no-nonsense judge acquitted me of a crime I absolutely committed.

I repeated the words out loud, but more like an idiot asking someone to repeat directions. "I don't have to do this anymore?"

I waited for Scottish bagpipes to strike up. They didn't. Nor did a scatterbrained flock of white doves come flapping like mad through every window, as if trespassing on the set of *The Birds*'s reboot or at a mafia wedding in New Jersey.

But something did happen. Gradually. Then suddenly.

Saying the statement out loud rattled awake a vegetative belief inside me, and I started slamming shut the open doors leading me to every logical reason to strike up a never-ending existential discussion in my head about who spoke to me.

Besides, thanks to my psychiatrist, I graded out as loony enough to objectively believe the words came straight from God. So, I chose to believe that's exactly who they came from.

And when I did, my thirty-year thirst vanished in a flash. I can't explain the disappearance any better than the space between an undiscovered galaxy a billion light-years away and the street corner where I stood, but imagining a scenario in which I ever wanted a drink again proved impossible to comprehend. And the thought of examining the miracle further, all the whats, whys, and hows, I concluded, would be a foolish waste of time, an undertaking more suited for the self-important bores of the world to stink up the only time we're given to call it home.

I wanted to mark this spot, if only for myself to preserve in my mind. Or to come back one day and share its meaning in the same way a veteran of war would by walking his loved ones over the soul-stained dirt atop a field where he battled with and lost dear friends, showing them the soil where his otherworldly gratitude and humility sprouted from after a lifetime of false starts, and make sure they leave with a clipped-off vine to nurture and grow, giving them a line to pull themselves out of whatever mess they got themselves into.

I peered back at the bench, a block back. Since I was loitering around in a residential neighborhood, I found it architecturally puzzling the bench wasn't in front of a house but rather a misplaced structure which somehow blended in with the postcard homes lining the street.

I walked back toward the building. Now the unconventional property stood out, looking much bigger. Indeed, this wasn't built for a single family or as a place to house additional first responders during avalanche and fire seasons. Perhaps a mansion rezoned for locals only. A place they kept to themselves, where they hung out, waiting as a local guru tuned up their skis and tossed back heavy shots of the town's best espresso while all the reviled tourists lined up at Starbucks atop the mountain like sheep for slaughter.

As I got closer, I took a few double takes and finally squinted my focus to confirm the building constituted none of these things. Instead, hiding in plain sight stood a church, the First Presbyterian of Telluride.

This prophetic sequence of hustle and bustle finally froze me stiff. And as the icy sting of understanding started to melt, my mind elevated above me, beyond me, now free from its demon's grip. Because this time, sounding more decided than individual notes plucked on a Lyon & Healy harp, I recognized an additional ethereal voice advising me—it was my dad, my Goddamn dad.

Son, you don't have to do this.

I could move again. I inhaled a lung full of fresh mountain air and held my breath, allowing the oxygen to settle in and expand. And I blew the sullied air out like a gust, blasting the stockpiles of accumulated metaphysical garbage I cowered behind the past thirty years, forever spoiling the view of salvation's path.

Now I saw it. Its surface appeared smooth, like mossy water on a still pond under the brightest of lights. This route lacked guardrails and stretched outward and onward into infinity. A road engineered with optimistic rigor, built to handle the weight of all comers.

But this road sat empty, unused by fellow travelers. As if created explicitly with me in mind for the journey God created me to take. I peered up to the only place authorized to build such a road.

"I don't have to drink anymore. No damn more."

And for the first time, I walked home without a thirst. Eager to reclaim life and salvage weathered bonds of love forsaken. Ready to stake the future on a fading mirage. Too astonished to consider my life should it ever fade to black.